THE SATIRE OF
THE THREE ESTATES

THE DRAMA LIBRARY

General Editor: Edward Thompson

THE SATIRE OF THE THREE ESTATES

by

SIR DAVID LINDSAY
OF THE MOUNT

Edinburgh Festival Version by
ROBERT KEMP

With an Introduction by
TYRONE GUTHRIE

WILLIAM HEINEMANN LTD
MELBOURNE :: LONDON :: TORONTO

To
Tyrone Guthrie

FIRST PUBLISHED
IN THE DRAMA LIBRARY
1951

PUBLISHED BY
WILLIAM HEINEMANN LTD
99 GREAT RUSSELL STREET, LONDON, W.C. 1
PRINTED IN GREAT BRITAIN AT
THE ST ANN'S PRESS, PARK ROAD, ALTRINCHAM

CONTENTS

Mr. Robert Kemp's version of *The Three Estates* was first produced by The Scottish Theatre in The Church of Scotland Assembly Hall, Edinburgh on 24th August, 1948, with the following cast:

DILIGENCE	A Herald	C. R. M. Brookes
KING HUMANITY		Bryden Murdoch
WANTONNESS		Douglas Campbell
PLACEBO	three courtiers	Peter MacDonell
SOLACE		James Stuart
SENSUALITY		Molly Urquhart
HOMELINESS		Jean Carrol
DANGER	her handmaids	Audrey Moncrieff
FUND-JENNETT	their porter	Dudley Stuart White
GOOD COUNSEL		Moultrie R. Kelsall
FLATTERY		Duncan Macrae
FALSEHOOD	three Vices	James Gibson
DECEIT		James Sutherland
VERITY		Lennox Milne
CHASTITY	two Virtues	Jean Taylor Smith
SPIRITUALITY	A Bishop	Andrew P. Wilson
PRIORESS		Edith Ruddick
ABBOT		Graham Squire
PARSON		Bruce Morgan
LORD TEMPORALITY		Robert McLauchlan
MERCHANT		John Main
SOUTAR		Jack Maguire
SOUTAR'S WIFE		Monty Landstein
TAILOR		William Young
TAILOR'S WIFE		Graham Squire
CORRECTION'S VARLET		Stanley Baxter
DIVINE CORRECTION		Ian Stewart
POOR MAN		Jack Lynn
PARDONER		Duncan Macrae
JOHN THE COMMON-WEAL		Archie Duncan
FIRST SERGEANT		Andrew Gray

SINGERS : TOWNSFOLK : SOLDIERS

The Music composed and directed by

CEDRIC THORPE DAVIE

The Costumes and Settings designed by

MOLLY MacEWEN

The Play produced by

TYRONE GUTHRIE

INTRODUCTION

by Tyrone Guthrie

FOR long enough Sir David Lindsay's *Satyre of the Thrie Estaites* lay neglected and, except to a few scholars, unknown. The reasons are not far to seek. It is enormously long, and the antiquity of its spelling (" quhilk " for " which ") makes it difficult to read.

The performances of Robert Kemp's version at the Edinburgh Festival in 1948, and at subsequent revivals, have aroused so much interest, that it may not be amiss to describe how they originated, and how this adaptation came to be made.

There had been some criticism of the first Edinburgh Festival programme because Scottish Art and Scottish artists had been insufficiently represented. The Committee recognized some truth in this, and felt that, without any departure from its original plan of a Festival of *international* character, some more importance might be allowed to native products, including Scottish Drama.

I was asked by the Festival Committee, when the second year's programme was being prepared, to direct a company of Scottish actors in a Scots play; if possible, a classic. Barrie, it was agreed, was not, at all events in the present epoch, whatever his future reputation may be, of classical status. Bridie was a member of the committee and did not wish his work considered. I was asked to read Home's *Douglas,* Ramsay's *Gentle Shepherd,* and *The Three Estates.*

Douglas is a dramatic curiosity, by reason of its history. But its extraordinary success in the XVIIIth century does not necessarily prove it a masterpiece. It only shows how greatly the taste of one epoch differs from that of another. An excellent and popular recent revival by the Citizen's Theatre, with Dame Sybil Thorndike in the leading part, has only confirmed me in this opinion. The revival was an interesting pastiche of byegone theatrical modes, and Dame Sybil's performance an impressive instance of how the tact and accomplishment of the actor can dominate an audience. But the play seemed, as one had always thought, a monotonous little melodrama in very conventional verse.

The Gentle Shepherd has immense charm; but it is a sort of Poetry Recital rather than a play; an elegant, intimate affair, leisured well-off townspeople being sentimental about The Country and the Good Poor. But to make a bold gesture in favour of Scottish Drama something larger and louder seemed to be required. I therefore sat down with a rather sinking heart to the two thick, squat, drab volumes of *The Three Estates*, with their teasing, difficult spelling, their columns of " Notes," their much needed Glossary.

For all its difficulties, it was soon apparent that Lindsay knew how to write for actors; and I thought that we had actors in Scotland who could do him justice. It seemed that, given three conditions, we might be able to make a " go " of it.

The three conditions were: first, a drastic abbreviation of the text and some adaptation to make it intelligible to the ordinary mortal, not just to the student of sixteenth century Scotland; second, the composition of suitable music; third, the finding of a suitable stage. I communicated all this to James Bridie, who represented the Festival Committee. He put me in touch with Robert Kemp, who consented to adapt the text.

Kemp and I were agreed that we must stick to the basic plan of Lindsay's work: that is to say, two main parts, the first dealing with moral and personal problems of conduct and conscience of the Individual, represented by King Humanity; the second, with the political and social problems of The Group. We decided that most of the theology must go, including a brilliant but enormously long sermon—three-quarters of an hour of unremitting pulpit-thumping at the penultimate stage of the evening.

Then there was the bawdery: between the allegory and the theology Lindsay had sandwiched a series of " Interludes." These are really knockabout sketches to be performed by members of the Lower Classes, and are a most striking and amusing contrast to the aristocratical and stately tone of the main body of the work. They are, however, by present-day standards, coarse and rough. We felt that in public performance, before mixed company, they might have caused more embarrassment than fun. But in any event the Lord Chamberlain's Office, with mantling cheek, would certainly have banned all the best " lines " and all the funniest " business." So all the Interludes were cut, save one, which, rather Bowdlerized, was kept in as a sort of specimen. It did not go very well in performance. Perhaps Dr. Bowdler was to blame!

Then the question had to be considered how far were we to keep Lindsay's magnificently highly-coloured attacks upon the Roman Church. The main target for his satire in the second part of the play is the contrast between the professions of the clergy and their practices. To eradicate this theme completely would be completely to emasculate the whole work.

We decided that any intelligent person, of whatever religious persuasion, must appreciate that the butt was not the Catholic Church, as such, but the Catholic Church at a particular epoch in a particular region; that the attack was not so much upon any particular

denomination as upon the whole idea of a great religious institu-
tion being abused by its officers for the furtherance of their private
interests. It is obvious that this is a danger which besets any impor-
tantly established religious organisation; equally obvious that the
Roman Catholic Church has, from time to time, through the
weakness of human nature laid itself open to this sort of charge;
equally obvious that it is not the only professedly Christian organisation so to do; one and all from time to time have used the Cross
as a Club to beat down opposition and silence the groans of the
oppressed.

In fact the performances aroused very little religious controversy.
There were some complaints by members of the Roman Catholic
community; but the Church authorities took a very broad and
tolerant line. And I think it is true to say that the vast majority of
those who saw the play appreciated that its religious satire is aimed,
not at Catholicism but at the frailty of parsonical human nature of
whatever denomination.

In general Mr. Kemp's task has been to abbreviate rather than
alter. But the cuts have had to be so drastic that there has often been
need of some sewing up of gaping wounds, and some smoothing of
raw edges. I hope that there may, through the years, be a few scholars
who will take the trouble carefully to collate this version with Lindsay's original. They may marvel at the squeamishness and hypocrisy
of this age, which deemed certain passages " indecent "; they may
disagree with some of the cuts and wish others more drastic; that is
inevitable. Tastes change with the passing years. But I feel there
will be few of these scholars who do not respect the modesty, humour
and integrity with which the lines and phrases of Kemp are blended
with those of Lindsay. There is more original Kemp in this edition
than one might suspect. Yet I defy anybody who has not both
versions before him to say where Lindsay ends and Kemp begins.

The version once made, it was shown to Mr. Thorpe Davie, who
was asked to provide music which should be now stately (for the
opening of the play, the arrival of King Humanity and so on); now
martial and stirring (for the entrance of Divine Correction, the
glorification of, and elevation to the Labour Peerage of John the
Commonweal); and now luscious and glamorous (the entrance of
Sensuality and the seduction of the King). All this was to be achieved
at minimal expense. It was; with the aid of three trumpets, some
drums and bells and an amateur chorus, who worked extremely
hard and well for " tea-money " and the glory of Scotland.

The third condition, the finding of a suitable stage, was fulfilled
after Kemp, Thorpe Davie, Bridie, William Grahame of the Festival
Office and myself had visited pretty well every public building in
Edinburgh. We sweated in Ballrooms, we froze in skating rinks, we
climbed to upper chambers where Ancient Buffaloes were wont to

meet of a Tuesday, by torchlight we felt our way through basements, we investigated dance halls, drill halls, school halls, church halls; halls large and small, beautiful, ugly, ancient and modern.

The sole piece of credit I take in connection with the whole business is that, when we came to the Kirk Assembly Hall, I knew we were home. Nobody else thought it suitable, but from the first moment I was convinced. That entrance, grim, black, forbidding but impressive, with its endless stone stairs, was just the right prelude to the play. The big square hall, with its wide low galleries around an arena, gave just the right possibilities for the sort of staging I had in mind. The general air of solid, smug, well-fed respectability, the sage-green upholstery, the stained glass, the corridors lined with sanitary tiling, the strong odour of sanctity, and the faint odour of gas; were all so sharply opposed to the whole spirit and feeling of the play, so gloriously wrong, that, perversely, I was convinced of their rightness. I begged to be allowed to risk the experiment. The Church authorities, to their great credit, agreed to let the hall. It largely conditioned the nature of the performance, and contributed to its striking and surprising success.

Perhaps it may be useful if I say something about the production. But I am not for one moment suggesting that the way we did the play was the Right Way. In art there is no single Right Way.

The play was given in the centre of the auditorium on a stage about twenty-five feet by fifteen feet, accessible from three of its four sides by shallow steps. The audience sat around three sides of the stage; behind the fourth side there was a gallery approached by stairs from the main stage. On this gallery sat the Spiritual Estate. Beneath it was a curtained recess, into which the King and Courtiers retired with Sensuality and her train. Nobles and Merchants sat in sort of jury boxes flanking this gallery. Entrances were made through the audience, down the aisles. The Three Estates were three groups of singers; their music was mostly contrapuntal.

In addition to these Three Estates we showed a Fourth—the disfranchised Poor, who took place at the end of the stage furthest from their noble and wealthy kinsmen. They lay in squalid rags on the steps and, as the mob always will, noisily supported whichever party seemed temporarily in the ascendant. At this end of the stage were set the stocks; and later the gallows.

The allegorical characters clearly lend themselves to many possible interpretations. Since the play seemed well able to take care of itself in the matter of dignity and grandeur, and since we had cut most of the broad comedy, I listed rather more heavily towards comedy than I think may have been Lindsay's intention. Good Counsel, for instance, was not just a good and wise man; he was a venerable, if lovable, bore. And Verity and Chastity were not two beautiful angels, they were two formidable dames—the former a lampoon upon the Lady Missionary, with a bible in one hand and a club in the other; the latter a sort of celestial Hospital Matron or Wardress, who moved with a crinkle of starched linen and a thump of stout boots. Their downfall at the hands of three endearing rogues (Flattery, Deceit and Falsehood) was consequently taken by the audience as a funny, not a pathetic, episode.

Through all the early stages of the play the sympathy of the audience was sought for the champions of Pleasure and Indecorum; so that the arrival of Divine Correction, built up to be as impressive as possible, suddenly swung the whole performance into an entirely new and serious key.

In the second part of the play a great table was set and the Estates were disposed as a sort of committee under the presidency of Divine Correction.

The speaking of the play presents some problems. Our experience was that the rhyme takes care of itself; but that rhythm must be carefully, but not ponderously, emphasized. It requires of the actors considerable speed of diction, and an ability to manage long phrases. It is death to the rhythm and vitality of the verse if the speaker pauses for breath at every comma, or at every line-end; often four and five lines must be ripped off at a breath.

So with all verse-plays, variety of pace and pitch and colour are essential. Nothing, in my view, does the poetic drama more disservice than the sort of reverence that decrees that the whole thing be spoken *andante moderato* in The Voice Beautiful.

PREFACE

by Robert Kemp

HAVING done some violence to Sir David Lindsay's *Satire of the Three Estates* by changing its language from Scots of the sixteenth century to Scots of the present day, and by somewhat reducing its length, I was unable to think of any good reason for refusing to take one further step, namely to prepare an English version. My excuse is that if those who find the Scottish version too difficult are now able to make something of an old play of the very greatest interest, I shall be the last to object. But purists may object. Therefore I must explain that the text which follows is a transcription into English, where possible, of another text, which was not offered to scholars but was prepared at the request of the Edinburgh Festival Committee for Mr. Tyrone Guthrie's production in the Church of Scotland's Assembly Hall in 1948. I hope that many who saw it at the Assembly Hall or who now read it will feel impelled to go back to Sir David Lindsay's original. If they choose to do so, they will find both the texts (the Bannatyne Manuscript of 1568 and the Charteris Quarto of 1602) printed in the Scottish Text Society's fine edition of the Works of Sir David Lindsay, while Mr. Douglas Hamer's introduction and notes give an admirable picture of Lindsay's life and times and of the circumstances surrounding the early performances of the *Satire*.

While we were conscious of the interest of the late Mr. James Bridie in the background, the chief architect of the *Satire*'s success was Mr. Tyrone Guthrie. The fates were clearly at their kindest in ordaining that the producer should be not only of international eminence but also, as of Scottish family and a past producer of the Scottish National Players, perculiarly fitted to understand the quirks of Sir David Lindsay's mind and the qualities of our Scottish actors. Those who worked under Mr. Guthrie were all conscious of a great opportunity. Because of the exhilaration that possessed them, they probably wasted few thoughts on the immeasurable harm that a failure would have done to their cause.

Before giving some account of the principles on which I worked, it would be well if I recalled the remarkable author of the *Satire* and the first performances of his play. In round terms, Sir David Lindsay was born in 1486 and died in 1555. He may well have been born at the Mount, the estate in Fife of which he later became the laird. It is possible that he studied at St. Andrews and certain that he served as a page at the brilliant court of King James the Fourth. There he took part in the masques which were arranged for the diversion of the king and his nobles. He does not seem to have been present at Flodden, although he stood near the king in St. Michael's Kirk, Linlithgow, when the " apparition " warned him against the fatal campaign. Perhaps because of his experience of dramatic illusions, Sir David has been suspected of having a hand in that prophetic manifestation. However that may be, he survived the disaster and became usher to the young King James the Fifth, whose infancy he recalls in some of the tenderest and most intimate lines of *The Complaint*.

In those days the herald fulfilled many of the duties of the diplomat of to-day and the Lyon King-of-Arms played a more important part in the affairs of state than may his tabarded successor whose presence on ceremonial occasions calls up so many visions of our past. Alliances were contracted by marriages between members of the reigning houses. Therefore when we read that Sir David was often entrusted with matrimonial bargaining on behalf of his king, we should think less of a connoisseur of feminine beauty than of a diplomat to whom that quality was among the less weighty recommendations for the position of Queen of Scots. In the power politics of the day the three most important figures were the Emperor Charles V, François I of France and Henry VIII of England. James was courted by all three and his choice of friends, particularly between the kings of France and England, had a daily bearing upon the survival of Scotland. Matrimonial missions made Sir David thoroughly acquainted with the court of Charles V at Brussels, and of François I in Paris and other towns of France. He visited Henry VIII of England and nearer the end of his life was an envoy to Denmark. David Beaton brought Marie de Lorraine home as the second French queen of James, but Lindsay had the welcoming of her at St. Andrews after she had landed at Crail.

He clearly led a life close to the centre of Scotland's affairs. He has also left us a fairly large body of poetry, which has for some time been neglected even by those who know their Dunbar and Henryson. It was not always so. The Scottish Text Society editor gives it as his opinion that Sir David was " the one Scottish poet before Burns who reached all classes, and reached them in a long series of editions unequalled by any poet before the close of the eighteenth century."

His greatest work is without doubt the *Satire*, which was first performed at Linlithgow Palace, probably in the Banqueting Hall, on Epiphany, 1540, before King James the Fifth and his Queen, Marie de Lorraine. A long and suggestive account of this occasion was sent to London by the English ambassador, but both the existing texts are identified with later performances—the Bannatyne with the performance at Cupar in 1552 and the Charteris with the Edinburgh performance of two years later. It is a credible theory that the first time the *Satire* was seen, it was an indoors play, concentrated in its action, and wanting in many of the comic features of later versions. If that is so, the Edinburgh version of 1948 may well have marked a return to something like the original play, more compact than the rambling public entertainment for a mediaeval holiday which has come down to us. But even going by the Charteris text, it is hard to see how the Edinburgh performance could last for the nine hours reported, unless there were long intervals for refreshment.

Sir David Lindsay's times seem remote from ours only at the first superficial glance. As soon as one looks more closely into them, their relevance to our own day grows and grows until it becomes astonishing. There was trouble in the East, for the capture of Constantinople by the Turks was one stage in a threat to Christendom as grave as any of the present time. Religious orthodoxy and accepted notions of every kind felt daily those hammer blows which we think peculiar to our own century. In astronomy the revolutionary notions of Copernicus were not only opening the way for navigation but were dislodging heaven and hell from their accepted positions in the universe. The shock must have equalled that of Darwinism. In the last decade of the fifteenth century came the wave of discoveries —of North America, of Brazil, of the sea route to India—of which the consequences are still being worked out. Italy was alive with the great impulses of the Renaissance, and Machiavelli was clarifying those principles of which, misapplied perhaps, the twentieth century had such a painful experience. Caxton's printing press at Westminster was ten years older than Sir David.

How far the author of the *Satire* was aware of some of these currents cannot be determined. He was much caught up in the greatest upheaval of all, the Reformation. Martin Luther was his elder by three years. In 1478 the Inquisition was established in Spain; in 1498 Savonarola was put to death in Florence. John Calvin and John Knox were both younger men than Lindsay, and though he probably met Knox at St. Andrews in 1547, neither can have influenced him as Luther clearly did. Rome was sacked by the mercenaries of Charles V in 1527; in 1534 Henry VIII of England rejected the supremacy of the Pope and dissolved the monasteries. The Society of Jesus was founded in the following year. Without carrying the comparison further, one may say that Luther cleft Europe almost as deeply as Lenin in the present age.

The *Satire*, then, is propaganda for the Reformation. Its preoccupations are the corruption of the clergy and their exactions from the poor. There is frequent reference to the New Testament in English, then circulating clandestinely in Scotland. It is beyond my ability to determine exactly where Sir David stood in relation to the religious conflict of his day. It is not denied, I think, that there was widespread alarm within the Roman Church—witness the remark of Cardinal Julian—and a body of opinion in favour of reform within the existing structure. Sir David may have been of that party, particularly if there is anything in the supposition that the Edinburgh performance took place at the request of Marie de Lorraine. It is reported that James V made the Linlithgow performance the occasion for lecturing some of the Scottish bishops about their ways. Although Sir David calls for far-reaching changes, he nowhere disowns the Pope. On the other hand it seems hard to believe that the lengths to which he carried his attack can have been pleasing to Marie, as they most certainly were not to the clergy, who ordered the burning of the Satire. Sir David was probably prepared to consider some more fundamental solution, although whether of the kind that came five years after his death, when Knox became supreme, no one can tell although each may guess according to his inclination.

The worldly prelate, high-living monk and fraudulent friar were already familiar to Chaucer's audience. Lindsay depicts them much more savagely, although at times with high-spirited humour, and without the gentler and more affectionate touches of the English poet. Only the Nun compelled by her " friends' greediness " to take vows is allowed to become human and worthy of sympathy. In Scotland, where David I, the " sair saint for the croun," had bestowed much crown land in the endowment of abbeys, it may be that a high number of men without religious vocation had entered the service of the Church. The jealousy which these lands excited in the no less cupidinous Scottish nobles played its part in the struggle of the day. Yet one of the greatest mysteries of the Satire lies in the fact that its performance was allowed, in an age that saw the burnings of Patrick Hamilton and George Wishart. Some have sought to find the reason in Lindsay's position near the king, but the two known open-air performances occurred during the regency of Marie.

The Satire of the Three Estates is a compound of morality play and political satire. The first half concerns the redemption of King Humanity from Sensuality and the Vices, which come in her train, by the sombre but majestic Divine Correction; in the second half the blemishes of the body politic and particularly ecclesiastic are exposed and " John the Commonweal," a representative figure of the people, is elevated to a place in the government of the kingdom. Here the reader may care to remember the similarity of Lindsay's views on kingship to those expressed in the Declaration of Arbroath. In this part comprehensive charges—of simony, plurality, oppression of the poor, illiteracy, lack of chastity—are preferred against the clergy. In the end, they are stripped of their fine vestments and driven off. In the original performances, they were shown to have fools' motley under their cassocks. This stripping is presumably symbolic of the removal of their possessions and privileges.

My problem in making the modern acting version were all of a practical nature. As someone wittily put it, I had to cut where the *Satire* was too long and too broad. It was clear that an audience of to-day did not want the whole thing and that it had to be reduced to something near the conventional time of two hours. If at the same time the number of characters—over forty in the original—could be reduced, it would be an advantage. It might fairly be claimed that Sir David would gain by cutting, for no one would deny that he can be long-winded and repetitive and that, especially where the Church is concerned, he will make a point over and over again. In the matter of breadth, not even the least squeamish would deny that some of his humour, thought to have been introduced for the diversion of the groundlings at the outdoor performances, could not be stomached by spectators of to-day. It was therefore necessary to leave out a great deal of this, but I kept in some of the rougher passages so that my version should even there give some feeling of the original.

There is a strong thread of action and argument running through the *Satire*. My guiding principle was to prune down to that action so that there should always be something happening on the stage. This was easy in the first half. In the second half, where the emphasis falls more upon argument and the whole convention is of a court of law or enquiry (surely this is an early example of the court scene) a greater degree of reorganization was needed. Here the most substantial cuts may be found but as they avoid repetitions and remove some of the plethora of characters they appeared to be justified. We left out completely the Folly episode after the hanging of the Vices. It contains many new characters and comes as an anti-climax. Perhaps I may note in passing that one result of my cutting was to reduce perhaps not the force of the attack on the Church, for that was part of the structure of the play, but certainly the extent of it.

My aim was to let Lindsay be heard and to write nothing at all myself. In cutting I aimed also at preserving the structure of Lindsay's verse—that is to say stanzas and couplets were removed whole but the pattern remained. It was possible on all but a very few occasions to observe both these rules. Sometimes cutting made it necessary to adjust the link; if part of a stanza had to be cut, I tried to transform it into another such as Lindsay might have used. These changes may be discernible by the small tooth comb method of comparison. I doubt if the ear could detect them.

Mr. Cedric Thorpe Davie, with whom I had often collaborated, was engaged to write the music, so that it was easy for me to imagine a musical punctuation which would give size and quality to the performance. Two songs are called for in the *Satire*, but there is no

B

record of words or tune. For these I introduced stanzas from the poets Scott and Montgomerie, both of the sixteenth century.

There was memorable pleasure in working under Mr. Guthrie on an old Scots play I admired on behalf of the city where I live. To know that among the actors and actresses there were many old friends, with whom I had often discussed some such occasion without really dreaming that we should live to see it come true—that was a reward which comes to few.

ROBERT KEMP

The Satire of the Three Estates

FIRST PART

There is a Fanfare of Trumpets and the members of the THREE ESTATES *of the Realm of Scotland enter singing. They are the* SPIRITUALITY *or Bishops, the* TEMPORALITY *or Barons and the* BURGESSES, *who are Merchants. They make their way on to the stage through the audience.*

ESTATES (*sing*): The Father, founder of faith and felicity,
That your fashion formèd to his similitude;
And his Son, our Saviour, shield in necessity,
That bought you from bane, ransomed on the Rood,
Re-pledging his prisoners with his heart-blood;
The Holy Ghost, governor and grounder of grace,
Of wisdom and welfare both fountain and flood,
Save you all that we see seated in this place,
        And shield you from sin,
And with His Spirit you inspire
Till we have shown our desire!
Silence, Sovereigns, we require,
        For now we begin!

(*During the singing* DILIGENCE, *a herald, has entered. He addresses the audience.*)

DILIGENCE: People, attend to me, and hold you coy![1]
Here am I sent to you, a messenger,
From a noble and right redoubted Roy,[2]
The which has been absent this many a year,
Who bade me show to you, but[3] variance,
That he intends among you to compear,
With a triumphant awful ordinance,
With crown and sword and sceptre in his hand,
Tempered with mercy when penitence appears;
Howbeit that he long time has been sleepand,[4]
Where through misrule has reigned these many years

[1] Quiet   [2] King   [3] without   [4] sleeping

And innocents been brought upon their biers
By false reporters of this nation . . .
Though young oppressors of their elders leirs[1]
Be now well sure of reformation!
(*A Fanfare.*)
And here by open proclamation,
I warn in name of his magnificence,
The Three Estatës of this nation,
That they compear with debtful diligence,
And to his grace make their obedience.
And first I warn the Spirituality,
And see the Burgesses spare not for expense,
But speed them here with Temporality!

(*As* DILIGENCE *names them,* SPIRITUALITY, TEMPOR-
ALITY *and the* MERCHANTS *take their places.*
DILIGENCE *turns to the audience again.*)

And I beseech you, famous auditors,
Convened into this congregation,
To be patient the space of certain hours,
Till you have heard our short narration.
Also we make you supplication
That no man take our words into disdain,
Howbeit you hear by lamentation,
The Common-Weal right piteously complain.
Prudent people, I pray you all,
Take no man grief in special;
For we shall speak in general,
    For pastime and for play.
Therefore, till all our rhymes be rung,
And our mis-tonèd songs be sung,
Let every man keep well one tongue,
    And every woman two!

(*A Fanfare and March. Young* KING HUMANITY
*enters with his train, chief among whom are two light-
hearted courtiers,* WANTONNESS *and* PLACEBO. *The*
ESTATES *sing* "Salve, rex humanitatis." *The*
KING *kneels before his throne.*)

KING: O Lord of lords, and King of kingës all,
Omnipotent of power, Prince but[2] peer
Eternal reigning in gloire celestial.
Unmade Maker, who, having no matter,
Made heaven and earth, fire, air and water clear
Send me thy grace with peace perpetual,
That I may rule my realm to thy pleasure;

        [1] learn   [2] without

Then bring my soul to joy angelical.
I thee request, who rent was on the Rood,
Me to defend from deedës of defame,
That my people report of me but good,
And be my safeguard both from sin and shame,
I know my days endure but as a dream;
Therefore, O Lord, heartily I thee exhort
To give me grace to use my diadem
To thy pleasure and to my great comfort.

(*The* KING *takes his seat on the throne.*)

WANTONNESS:
My Sovereign Lord and Prince but peer,
Why do you make such dreary cheer?
Be blithe so long as you are here,
 And pass time with pleasure:
For as long lives the merry man
As the sorry, for ought he can.
His bones full sore, sir, shall I ban[1]
 That does you displeasure.
So long as Placebo and I
Remain into your company,
Your grace shall live right merrily,
 Of this have you no doubt!
So long as you have us in cure,
Your grace, sir, shall want no pleasure:
Were Solace here, I you assure,
 He would rejoice this rout!

PLACEBO:
Good brother mine, where is Solace,
The mirror of all merriness?
I have great marvel, by the Mass,
 He's tarrying so long.
Bide he away, we are but shent![2]
I wonder how he from us went.
I trow he has impediment
 That lets him not to gang.

WANTONNESS:
I left Solace, that same great loon,
Drinking into the borough's town—
It will cost him half-a-crown
 Although he had no more!
Also he said he would go see
Fair Lady Sensuality,
The beryl of all beauty
 And portraiture preclair.

(*Enter* SOLACE, *the third Courtier, running.*)
  [1] curse   [2] lost

PLACEBO:
By God, I see him at the last,
As he were chased running right fast;
He glares, even as he were aghast,
Or frightened by a ghost . . .

(SOLACE, *drunk, at first addresses the audience.*)

SOLACE:
Wow! Who saw ever such a throng?
Methought some said I had gone wrong.
Had I help, I would sing a song
With a right merry noise!
I have such pleasure in my heart
That makes me sing the treble part—
Would some good fellow fill the quart?
That would my heart rejoice!
What is my name? Can ye not guess?
Sirs, know you not Sandy Solace?
They called my mother Bonny Bess
That dwelled between the Bows.
At twelve years old she learned to swyve,
Thankèd be thou, great god of life,
She made me fathers four or five—
But doubt, this is no mows![1]
And if I lie, sirs, ye may spier[2]
But saw you not the King come here?
I am a sporter and play-fere[3]
To that young King.
He said he would, within short space,
To pass his time come to this place—
I pray to God to give him grace
And long to reign.

KING:
My servant Solace, what made you tarry?

(SOLACE *suddenly sees him.*)

SOLACE:
I wot not, sir, by sweet Saint Mary;
I have been in a fairy-fairy
Or else into a trance!
Sir, I have seen, I you assure,
The fairest earthly creature,
That ever was formèd by nature
And most for to advance.
To look on her is great delight
With lips so red and cheeks so white,
I would renounce all this world quite
To stand into her grace!

[1] no joke   [2] ask   [3] mate

She is wanton and she is wise,
And clad she is in the new guise—
It would make all your flesh up-rise
 To look upon her face.
Were I a king, it should be kend,
I would not spare on her to spend
And this same night for her to send
 For my pleasure!
What rack of your prosperity,
If you want Sensuality?
I would not give a silly fly
 For your treasure!

KING: Forsooth, my friends, I think you are not wise,
To counsel me to break commandement
Directed by the Prince of Paradise;
Considering you know that mine intent
Is for to be to God obedient,
Who does forbid men to be lecherous.
Do I not so, perchance I shall repent.
Therefore I think your counsel odious.
 The which you gave me till.[1]
Because I have been to this day
Tanquam tabula rasa
 Ready for good and ill.

PLACEBO: Believe you that we will beguile you,
Or from your virtue we will wile you,
Or with our evil words defile you
 Both into good and evil?
To take your grace's part we grant,
In all your deeds participant,
So that you be not a young saint
 And then an old devil.

WANTONNESS: Believe you, sir, that lechery be sin?
No, trow not that! This is my reason why.
First at the Roman Court will you begin,
Which is the gleaming lamp of lechery,
Where cardinals and bishops generally
To love ladies they think a pleasant sport
And out of Rome have banished Chastity,
Who with our prelates can get no resort!

SOLACE: Until you get a prudent queen,
I think your Majesty serene

[1] to

Should have a lusty concubine
    To play you with all:
For I know, by your quality,
You lack the gift of chastity.
Fall to, *in nomine Domini*!
    For this is my counsel!
I speak, sir, under protestation
That none at me have indignation,
For all the prelates of this nation
    For the most part,
They think no shame to have a whore
And some have three under their cure—
This to be true I'll you assure,
    You shall hear afterward.
Sir, knew you all the matter through.
    To play you would begin.
Ask at the monks of Balmerino
    If lechery be sin!

PLACEBO: Sir, send forth Sandy Solace,
Or else your minion Wantonness
And pray my Lady Prioress
    The sooth to declare,
If it be sin to take a Katie
Or to live like a Bummilbaty.[1]
The Book says " *Omnia probate* "
    And not for to spare!

(*Music*. LADY SENSUALITY *enters accompanied by
her maidens* HOMELINESS *and* DANGER, *and by* FUND-
JENNET, *a porter. They take up their position at the
end of the stage remote from the* KING *and his
courtiers, who do not see them.*)

SENSUALITY: Lovers awake! Behold the fiery sphere,
Behold the natural daughter of Venus!
Behold, lovers, this lusty lady clear,
The fresh fountain of knightës amorous,
Replete with joys, douce and delicious.
Or who would make to Venus observance
In my mirthful chamber melodious?
There shall they find all pastime and pleasance.
Behold my head, behold my gay attire,
Behold my neck, lovesome and lily-white;
Behold my visage flaming as the fire,
Behold my paps, of portraiture perfite!
            [1] booby

To look on me lovers have great delight;
Right so have all the kings of Christendom—
To them I have done pleasures infinite
And specially unto the Court of Rome.
One kiss of me were worth, in one morning,
A million of gold to knight or king.
And yet I am of nature so toward
I let no lover pass with a sore heart.
Of my name, would you know the verity?
Forsooth they call me Sensuality.
I hold it best now, ere we further gang,
To Dame Venus let us go sing a song.

HOMELINESS: Madame, no tarrying
We shall fall to and sing.
Sister Danger, come near!

DANGER: Sister, sing this song I may not,
Without the help of good Fund-Jennet,
Fund-Jennet, ho! Come take a part!

FUND-JENNET: That shall I do with all my heart!
Sister, howbeit that I am hoarse,
I am content to hear a bass.
You two should love me as your life—
You know I learned you both to swyve
In my chamber, you know well where,
Since then the fiend a man you spare!

HOMELINESS: Fund-Jennet, fie, you are to blame!
To speak foul words, think you not shame?

FUND-JENNET: There are a hundred sitting by
That love japing as well as I,
Might they get in it privity—
But who begins the song, let's see!

(*They sing verses from the poem by Alexander Montgomerie.*)

Hey, now the day daws,
The jolly cock crows,
Now shroudes the shaws[1]
    Through Nature anon.
The thissel-cock cries
On lovers that lies,
Now skailes[2] the skies,
    The night is near gone.
    [1] woods   [2] empties

The fields overflows
With gowans that grows
Where lilies like lowe[1] is,
 As red as the roan;
The turtle that true is,
With notes that renews,
Her party pursues,
 The night is near gone!

Now harts with their hinds
Conform to their kinds,
High tosses their tynds[2]
 On ground where they groan,
Now hedge-hogs, with hares,
Aye passes in pairs,
Which duly declares
 The night is near gone.

The season excels
Through sweetness that smells;
Now Cupid compels
 Our hearts everyone,
On Venus who wakes
To muse on our maiks[3]
Then sing for their sakes
 The night is near gone!

(*During the singing of the song the* KING *and his court see* SENSUALITY *and her party.*)

KING:

Up, Wantonness, thou sleeps too long!
Methought I heard a merry song.
I thee command in haste to gang,
See what yon mirth may mean!

WANTONNESS:

I trow, sir, by the Trinity,
Yon same is Sensuality,
If it be so, soon shall I see
 That sovereign serene!

PLACEBO:

Sir, she is greatly to advance,
For she can both play and dance,
That perfect patron of pleasance,
 A pearl of pulchritude!
Soft as the silk is her white lyre,[4]
Her hair is like the golden wire,
My heart burns in a flame of fire
 I swear you by the Rood.

  [1] flame [2] antlers [3] mates [4] skin

SOLACE: What say you, sir? Are you content
That she come here incontinent?
What 'vails your kingdom and your rent
    And all your great treasure,
Without you have a merry life,
And cast aside all sturt and strife?
And so long as you lack a wife,
    Fall to, and take your pleasure!

KING: Forsooth, I wot not how it stands,
But since I heard of your tidings,
My body trembles, feet and hands,
    And whiles is hot as fire!
I trow Cupido with his dart
Has wounded me out-through the heart;
My spirit will from my body part,
    Get I not my desire!
Pass on, away, with diligence,
And bring her here to my presence!
Spare not for travel or expense,
    I care not for no cost!
Pass on your way soon, Wantonness,
And take with you Sandy Solace,
And bring that Lady to this place,
    Or else I am but lost!
Commend me to that sweetest thing,
Present her with this same rich ring,
And say I lie in languishing,
    Except she make remede!
With sighing sore I am but shent[1]
Without she come incontinent
My heavy languor to relent
    And save me now from deid![2]

WANTONNESS: Doubt you not, sir, but we will get her,
We shall be fiery for to fetch her,
But, faith, we would speed all the better,
    Had I more than a plack![3]

SOLACE: Sir! Let not sorrow in you sink,
But give us ducats for to drink
And we shall never sleep a wink
    Till we have brought her back!

(THE KING *gives them a purse.*)

KING: I pray you, speed you soon again!

        [1] lost   [2] death   [3] halfpenny

WANTONNESS: Yea, of this song, sir, we are fain!
                We shall neither spare for wind nor rain
                    Till our day's work be done!
                Farewell, for we are at the flight!
                Placebo, rule our Roy aright—
                We shall be here, man, ere midnight
                    Though we march with the moon!

                (*A gay march.* SOLACE *and* WANTONNESS *make a
                detour of the stage and come to* SENSUALITY *and her
                court.*)

                Pastime with pleasure and great prosperity
                Be to you, Sovereign Sensuality!

SENSUALITY: Sirs, you are welcome. Where go you? East or
                    West?

WANTONNESS: In faith, I trow we be at the farthest!

SENSUALITY: What is your name? I pray, sir, declare!

WANTONNESS: Marry, Wantonness, the King's secretair.

SENSUALITY: What king is that, who has so gay a boy?

WANTONNESS: Humanity, that rich redoubted Roy,
                Who does commend him to you heartfully,
                And sends you here a ring with a ruby,
                In token that above all creature
                He has chosen you to be his Paramour:
                He bade me say that he will be but dead,
                Without that you make hastily remede.

SENSUALITY: How can I help him, though he should fore-fare?[1]
                You know right well I'm no Mediciner.

SOLACE: A kiss of your sweet mouth, in a morning,
                To his sickness might be great comforting.
                Also he makes you supplication
                This night to make with him collation.

SENSUALITY: I thank his grace of his benevolence!
                Good sirs, I shall be ready out of hand.
                In me there shall be found no negligence,
                Both night and day, when his grace will demand.
                Pass you before, and say I am comand[2]
                And think right long to have of him a sight.
                And I to Venus make a faithful bond
                That in his arms I think to lie all night.
                    [1] perish   [2] coming

WANTONNESS: That shall be done . . . but yet ere I home pass,
Here I protest for Homeliness, your lass.

SENSUALITY: She shall be at command, sir, when you will:
I trust she shall you find flinging your fill!

WANTONNESS: Now hey for joy and mirth I dance!
(*Music, which accompanies the speech.*)
Take there a gay gamond[1] of France!
Am I not worthy to advance
　　That am so good a page,
And that so speedily can run
To 'tice my master unto sin?
The fiend a penny he will win
　　Of this his marriage!

(*A dance, during which* WANTONNESS *and* PLACEBO
skip back to the KING. *On the way* WANTONNESS
pretends to hurt his leg.)

WANTONNESS (*to audience*): I think this day to win great thank!
Hey, as a bridled cat I brank![2]
Alas, I have wrested[3] my shank . . .
　　Yet I gang, by St. Michael.
Which of my legs, sir, as you trow,
Was it that I did hurt even now?
But whereto should I ask at you—
　　I think they both are whole!
(*He turns to the* KING. *The music ends.*)
Good morrow, Master, by the Mass!

KING: Welcome, my minion Wantonness!
How hast thou sped on thy travel?

WANTONNESS: Right well, by Him that harried hell!
Your errand is well done!

KING (*transported*): Then, Wantonness, full well is me!
Thou hast deserved both meat and fee,
　　By Him that made the moon!
(*anxiously*): There is one thing that I would
　　spier . . .[4]
What shall I do when she comes here?
For I know not the craft perqueir[5]
　　Of lovers' gin;
Therefore at length you must me leir[6]
　　How to begin.

　　[1] caper　　[2] prance　　[3] sprained　　[4] ask　　[5] by heart　　[6] learn

WANTONNESS:　To kiss her and clap her, sir, be not affeared!
　　　　　　　She will not skrink though you kiss her a span
　　　　　　　　　within the beard.
　　　　　　　If you think she thinks shame, then hide the bairn's
　　　　　　　　　head
　　　　　　　With her train, and tend her well, you wot what I
　　　　　　　　　mean!
　　　　　　　Will you give me leave, sir, first to go to,
　　　　　　　And I shall learn you the cues how to do?

KING:　　　　God forbid, Wantonness, that I give you leave!
　　　　　　　Your are too perilous a page such practice to
　　　　　　　　　prove!

　　　　　　　(WANTONNESS *sees* SENSUALITY.)

WANTONNESS:　Now, sir, prove as you please, I see her comand![1]
　　　　　　　Order you with gravity, we shall by you stand!

　　　　　　　(*Music. The* KING *and his courtiers prepare to
　　　　　　　welcome* SENSUALITY. *She apart first takes her vow
　　　　　　　to Venus, accompanied by music.*)

SENSUALITY:　O Venus goddess, unto thy celsitude
　　　　　　　I give laud, gloire, honour and reverence,
　　　　　　　Who granted me such perfect pulchritude,
　　　　　　　That princes of my person have pleasance,
　　　　　　　I make a vow, with humble observance,
　　　　　　　That I will in thy temple visit thee
　　　　　　　With sacrifice unto thy deity!
　　　　　　　(*She turns towards the* KING.)
　　　　　　　And now my way I must advance
　　　　　　　Unto a prince of great puissance,
　　　　　　　Who young men has in governance,
　　　　　　　　　Rolling into his rage.
　　　　　　　I am right glad, I you assure,
　　　　　　　That potent prince to get in cure,
　　　　　　　Who is of lustings the lure
　　　　　　　　　And greatest of courage.

　　　　　　　(*The music ends. A detour brings her at last to the*
　　　　　　　KING.)

　　　　　　　O potent prince, of pulchritude preclair,
　　　　　　　God Cupido preserve your celsitude!
　　　　　　　May the dame Venus keep your court from care,
　　　　　　　As I would she should keep my own heart blood!

KING:　　　　Welcome to me, peerless of pulchritude!
　　　　　　　Welcome to me, thou sweeter than the amber,
　　　　　　　　　　　　[1] coming

	Who may of all my dolour me denude!
	Solace, convoy this lady to my chamber!
SENSUALITY:	I go this gait[1] with right good will.
	Sir Wantonness, tarry you still?
	Let Homeliness the cup you fill
	And bear you company!

(*Music, which continues till the departure of* KING *and party.*)

HOMELINESS:	That shall I do without a doubt,
	For he and I shall play cap-out!
WANTONNESS:	Now lady, let me have turn about,
	Fill in for I am dry!
	Your dame, by now, truly,
	Has gotten upon her keel!
	What rack though you and I
	Go join the joust as well?
HOMELINESS:	Content I am with right good will,
	Whenever you are ready,
	All your pleasure to fulfill.
WANTONNESS:	Now well said, by our Lady!
	I'll bear my master company,
	As long as I endure!
	If he be whisking wantonly,
	We shall fling on the floor!

(*The* KING *and his party go into the arbour at the top of the stage. As they disappear* GOOD COUNSEL, *a bearded figure hobbles in and addresses the audience.*)

GOOD COUNSEL:	Consider, my sovereigns, I you beseech,
	The cause most principal of my coming.
	Princes or potestates are not worth a leek,
	Be they not guided by my good governing.
	There was never emperor, conqueror nor king,
	Without my wisdom that might their weal advance.
	My name is Good Counsel, without feigning;
	Lords for lack of my law are brought to mischance.
	And so, for conclusion,
	Who guide them not by Good Counsel,
	All in vain is their travail,
	And finally fortune shall them fail,
	And bring them to confusion
	And this I understand,
	For I have my residence

[1] way

With high princes of great puissance,
In England, Italy and France,
　　And many other land.
But out of Scotland, alas,
I have been banished long space——
That makes our guiders all lack grace,
And die before their day!
Because they lightly[1] Good Counsel,
Fortune turned on them her sail,
Which brought this realm to greatest bale[2]——
　　Who can the contrair say?
My lords, I came not here to lie;
Woes me for King Humanity,
O'erset with Sensuality
　　In his first beginning,
Through vicious counsel insolent!
So they mày get riches or rent
To his welfare they take no tent,[3]
　　Nor what shall be the ending!
But would the King be guided yet with reason
And on mis-doers make punition,
Howbeit that I long time have been exiled
I trust in God my name shall yet be styled,
So till I see God send more of his grace,
I purpose to repose me in this place.
(GOOD COUNSEL *draws apart.* FLATTERY, *the first
of the Three Vices to appear, rushes in, dressed in
motley.*)

FLATTERY:　　Make room, sirs, ho! that I may run!
Lo, see how I am new come in,
　　Begaried[4] all with sundry hues!
Let be your din till I begin,
　　And I shall show you of my news!
Throughout all Christendom I have passed
And am come here now at the last,
Stormstayed on sea aye since Yule Day,
That we were fain to hew our mast,
Not half a mile beyond the May.[5]
But now among you I will remain,
I purpose never to sail again,
　　To put my life in chance of water.
Was never seen such wind and rain,
　　Nor of shipmen such clitter-clatter.
Some bade " Hail! " and some bade " Stand-by! "
" On starboard ho! " " A-luff, fie, fie! "

[1] disdain　　[2] sorrow　　[3] heed　　[4] bedecked　　[5] May Island

> Till all the ropes began to rattle,
> Was never wight so fley't[1] as I,
>   When all the sails played brittle-brattle!
> To see the waves, it was a wonder,
> And wind, that rave the sails in sunder!
> Now am I 'scaped from that affray;
> What say you, sirs, am I not gay?
>   Know you not Flattery, your own fool,
> That went to make this new array?
>   Was I not here with you at Yule?
> Yes, by my faith, I think so well!
> Where are my fellows that would not fail?
>   We should have come here for a cast!
> Ho, Falsehood, ho!

(FALSEHOOD enters.)

FALSEHOOD: We serve the Deil![2]
     Who's that that cries for me so fast?

FLATTERY: Why, Falsehood, brother, know thou not me?
     I am thy brother, Flattery!

FALSEHOOD: Now let me brace thee in my arms,
     When friend meets friend, the heart aye warms!

(They embrace.)

FLATTERY: Where is Deceit, that limmer loon?[3]

FALSEHOOD: I left him drinking in the town,
     He will be here incontinent.

FLATTERY: Now by the Holy Sacrament,
     These tidings comfort all my heart!
     He is right crafty as you ken,
     And counsellor to the Merchant-men!

(Enter DECEIT.)

DECEIT: Bon jour, brother, with all my heart,
     Here am I come to take your part
      Both into good and evil!
     I met Good Counsel by the way,
     Who put me in a felon fray[4]—
      I give him to the devil!
     How came you here, I pray you tell me!

FALSEHOOD: Marry, to seek King Humanity!

[1] scared [2] Devil [3] scoundrel [4] fright

C

DECEIT: Now, by the good lady that me bare,
                That same horse is my own mare!
                Since we three seek yon noble King,
                Let us devise some subtle thing!
                Also I pray you as your brother,
                That we, each one, be true to other.
                I pray to God, nor I be hanged,
                But I shall die ere you be wronged!

FALSEHOOD: What is thy counsel that we do?

DECEIT: Marry, sirs, this is my counsel, lo!
                From time the King begins to stir him,
                I dread Good Counsel may come near him,
                And be we known to Lord Correction,
                It will be our confusion.
                Therefore, my dear brother, devise
                To find some toy of the new guise.

FLATTERY: Marry, I shall find a thousand wiles.
                We must turn our clothes, and change our styles
                And so disguise us, that no man know us.
                Has no man clerk's clothing to lend us?
                And let us keep grave countenance,
                As we were new come out of France!

DECEIT: Now, by my soul, that is well devised!
                You'll see me soon right well disguised.

FALSEHOOD: And so shall I, man, by the Rood!
                Now, some good fellow, lend me a hood!

                (*The* THREE VICES *disguise themselves in clothes
                from a bundle which* DECEIT *has brought on.*)

DECEIT: Now am I busked, and who can spy?
                The devil stick me, if this be I!
                If this be I, or not, I cannot well say,
                Or has the Fiend of Fairy-folk borne me away?

FALSEHOOD: What say you of my gay garmoun?[1]

DECEIT: I say you look even like a loon.
                Now, brother Flattery, what do you?
                What kind of man shape you to be?

FLATTERY: Now, by my faith, my brother dear,
                I will go counterfeit a friar!

DECEIT: A friar? Whereto you cannot preach?

                                    [2] garment

FLATTERY: What rack, if I can flatter and fleech?[1]
Perchance I'll come to that honour,
To be the King's confessor.
Poor friars are free at any feast
And marshalled aye among the best!

(DECEIT *has fetched a monk's cowl.*)

DECEIT: Here is thy gaining, all and some,
That is a cowl of Tullilum!

FLATTERY: Who has a breviary to lend me?
The fiend a soul, I trow, will ken me!

(*The* BISHOP *tosses down a breviary.*)

FALSEHOOD: We must do more yet, by St. James!
For we must all three change our names.
Christen me and I shall baptise thee.

(*There follows a mock ceremony.*)

DECEIT: By God and thereabout may it be!
How will you call me, I pray you tell!

FALSEHOOD: I wot not how to call mysel'!

DECEIT: But yet once name the bairn's name!

FALSEHOOD: Discretion, Discretion in God's name!

DECEIT: I need not now to care for thrift,
But what shall be my Godbairn gift?

FALSEHOOD: I give you all the devils of hell!

DECEIT: No, brother, hold that to yoursel'!
Now, sit down! Let me baptise thee!
I wot not what thy name should be.

FALSEHOOD: But yet once name the bairn's name!

DECEIT: Sapience, Sapience, in God's name!

FLATTERY: Brother Deceit, come baptise me!

DECEIT: Then sit down lowly on thy knee!

FLATTERY: Now, brother, name the bairn's name.

DECEIT: Devotion in the devil's name.

(*He splashes* FLATTERY *with water.*)
[1] wheedle

FLATTERY: The deil receive thee, lurdan loon![1]
            Thou has wet all my new shaven crown!

ALL: Devotion, Sapience, and Discretion—
            We three may rule this region.
            We shall find many crafty things
            For to beguile a hundred kings!

DECEIT   (*to* FALSEHOOD): For thou can right well crack and
                         clatter,
            And I shall feign and (*to* FLATTERY) thou shalt
                         flatter.

FLATTERY: But I would have, ere we departed,
            A drink to make us better hearted.

DECEIT: Well said, by Him that harried hell,
            I was even thinking that mysel'!

            (*While the* THREE VICES *are drinking, the* KING
            appears leading SENSUALITY *from the arbour.*)

KING: Now where is Placebo and Solace?
            Where is my minion Wantonness?
            Wantonness, ho! Come to me soon!

            (WANTONNESS *and* HOMELINESS *appear.*)

WANTONNESS: Why cried you, sir, till I had done?

KING: What were you doing, tell me that?

WANTONNESS: Marry, learning how my father me got!
            I wot not how it stands, but[2] doubt
            Methinks the world runs round about!

KING: And so think I, man, by my thrift!
            I see fifteen moons in the lift.[3]

            (SOLACE, PLACEBO *and* DANGER *appear.*)

SOLACE: Now show me, sir, I you exhort,
            How are you of your love content?
            Think you not this a merry sport?

KING: Yea, that I do in verament![4]

            (*The* KING *spies the* THREE VICES.)

            What bairns are yon upon the bent?
            I did not see them all this day.

[1] rogue   [2] without   [3] sky   [4] truth

WANTONNESS:	They will be here incontinent. Stand still and hear what they will say.
	(*The* THREE VICES *come forward and salute the* KING.)
VICES:	Laud, honour, gloire, triumph and victory, Be to your most excellent Majesty!
KING:	You are welcome, good friends, by the Rood! Apparently you seem some men of good. What are your names, tell me without delay!
DECEIT:	Discretion, sir, is my name perfray.
KING:	What is your name, sir, with the clippèd crown?
FLATTERY:	But doubt, my name is called Devotion.
KING:	Welcome, Devotion, by Saint Jame! Now, sirrah, tell what is your name?
FALSEHOOD:	Marry, sir, they call me . . . what call they me? (*Aside*) I wot not well, but if I lie!
KING:	Can you not tell what is your name?
FALSEHOOD:	I knew it when I came from home!
KING:	What ails you cannot show it now?
FALSEHOOD	(*confused*): Marry, they call me Thin-Drink, I trow!
KING:	Thin-Drink, what kind of name is that?
DECEIT:	Sapience, thou serves to bear a plate! Methinks thou shows thee not well-witted.
FALSEHOOD:	Sypiens, sir, Sypiens, marry now you hit it! (FLATTERY *brushes* FALSEHOOD *aside*.)
FLATTERY:	Sir, if you please to let me say, That same is Sapientia!
FALSEHOOD:	That same is it, by St. Michael!
KING:	Why could thou not tell it thysel'?
FALSEHOOD:	I pray your grace to pardon me. And I shall show the verity— I am so full of Sapience That sometimes I will take a trance!
KING:	Sapience should be a man of good.
FALSEHOOD:	Sir, you may know that by my hood!

KING:

Now have I Sapience and Discretion,
How can I fail to rule this region?
And Devotion to be my Confessor!
These three came in a happy hour.
(*to* FALSEHOOD) Here I make thee my secretar!
(*to* DECEIT) And thou shalt be my treasurer!
(*to* FLATTERY) And thou shalt be my counsellor
In spiritual things, and confessor.

FLATTERY:

I swear to you, sir, by St. Ann,
You never met a wiser man,
For many a craft, sir, do I can,
     Were they well known.
I have no feel of flattery,
But fostered with philosophy,
A strong man in astronomy,
Which shall be soon shown!

FALSEHOOD:

And I have great intelligence,
In quelling of the quintessence,
But to prove my experience,
     Sir, lend me forty crowns!
To make multiplication,
And take my obligation—
If we make false narration,
     Hold us for very loons!

DECEIT:

Sir, I know by your physnomy,
You shall conquer, or else I lie,
Danskin,[1] Denmark and Almane,
Spitalfield and the Realm of Spain.
You shall have at your governance
Renfrew and the Realm of France,
Yea, Ru'glen and the Town of Rome,
Corstorphine and all Christendom.
Whereto, sir, by the Trinity,
You are a very A per se.

FLATTERY:

Sir, when I dwelt in Italy,
I learned the craft of palmistry.
Show me the palm, sir, of your hand,
And I shall make you understand
If your grace be unfortunate
Or if you be predestinate.

(*The* KING *shows his hand.*)

I see you will have fifteen queens
[1] Dantzig

And fifteen score of concubines!
The Virgin Mary save your grace,
Saw ever man so white a face,
So great an arm, so fair a hand,
Or such a leg in all this land!
Were you in arms, I think no wonder,
Howbeit you struck down fifteen hundred.

KING: You are right welcome, by the Rood!
         You seem to be three men of good!

(GOOD COUNSEL *takes up a more prominent position.*)

But who is yon that stands so still?
Go spy and ask what is his will.
And if he yearns of my presence,
Bring him to me with diligence.

(*The* THREE VICES *quickly confer.*)

FLATTERY: I doubt full sore by God himsel'
             That yon old carl be Good Counsel!
             Get he once to the King's presence,
             We three will get no audience!

DECEIT: That matter I shall take on hand,
           And say it is the King's command,
           That he anon avoid this place,
           And come not near the King his grace,
           And that under the pain of treason!

FLATTERY: Brother, I hold your counsel reason.
             Now let us hear what he will say.

(*He addresses* GOOD COUNSEL.)

Old lyart[1] beard, good day, good day!

GOOD COUNSEL: Good day again, sirs, by the Rood!
                 I pray God make you men of good.

DECEIT: Pray not for us to Lord nor Lady,
           For we are men of good already!
           Sir, show to us what is your name.

GOOD COUNSEL: Good Counsel they call me at home.

FALSEHOOD: What sayest thou, carl, art thou Good Counsel?
              Swift, pack thee hence, unhappy mortal!

GOOD COUNSEL: I pray you, sirs, give me licence,
                 [1] hoary

To come once to the King's presence
To speak but two words to his grace.

FLATTERY: Quick, whoreson carl, devoid this place!

GOOD COUNSEL: Brother, I know you well enough,
Howbeit you make it never so tough—
Flattery, Deceit and False-Report
That will not suffer to resort
Good Counsel to the King's presence.

DECEIT: Swift, whoreson carl, go pack thee hence!
If ever thou come this gait[1] again,
I vow to God thou shalt be slain!

(*They set upon* GOOD COUNSEL *and push him from the stage.*)

GOOD COUNSEL: Since at this time I can get no presence,
Is no remede but take in patience.
But when youth-head has blown his wanton blast,
Then shall Good Counsel rule him at the last!

(GOOD COUNSEL *is chased out. The* THREE VICE *return to the* KING.)

KING: What made you bide so long from my presence?
I think it long since you departed thence.
What was yon man, with a great bousteous beard?
Methought he made you all three very feared!

DECEIT: It was a loathly lurdan loon,
Come to break booths into this town!
We have caused bind him to a pole
And send him to the Thieves' Hole.

KING: Let him sit there with a mischance!
And let us go to our pastimes!

WANTONNESS: Better go revel at the racket,
Or else go to the hurley-hacket,[2]
Or then to show our courtly courses,
Go see who best can run their horses!

(*As they make to move* SOLACE *stops them.*)

SOLACE: No, Sovereign, ere we further gang,
Let Sensuality sing a song.

(*They sing verses from a poem by Alexander Scott.*)
           [1] way   [2] a game

To love unlovèd is a pain,
For she that is my sovereign
   Some wanton man so he has set her
That I can get no love again,
   But breaks my heart, and nought the better!

When that I went with that sweet may
To dance, to sing, to sport and play,
   And ofttimes in my arms to plait her
I do now mourn both night and day
   And breaks my heart and nought the better!

What a poor glaikit[1] fool am I,
To slay myself with melancholy,
   Since well I know I may not get her!
Or what should be the cause, and why
   To break my heart and nought the better!

My heart, since thou may not her please,
Adieu! As good love comes as goes!
   Go choose another and forget her!
God give him dolour and disease
   That breaks their heart, and nought the better!

(*As the music ends,* VERITY *enters, a Puritan maid holding a Bible. She stands apart but* FLATTERY *goes out to peer at her as she speaks.*)

VERITY: If men of me would have intelligence,
Or know my name, they call me Verity.
Of Christës law I have experience,
And have o'er sailèd many a stormy sea.
Now I am seeking King Humanity;
For of his grace I have good esperance.
From time that he acquainted be with me,
His honour and high gloire I shall advance.

(*As* FLATTERY *returns* DECEIT *greets him.*)

DECEIT: Good day, Father, where have you been?
Declare to us of your novelles.

FLATTERY: There is now lighted on the green,
Dame Verity, by books and bells!
But come she to the King's presence,
There is no boot for us to bide!
Therefore I rede us, all go hence!

FALSEHOOD: That will be not yet, by St. Bride!
But we shall either gang or ride
      [1] simple

To Lords of Spirituality,
And make them trow yon bag of pride
Has spoken manifest heresy!

(*Here the* THREE VICES *go to the* SPIRITUAL ESTATE.)

FLATTERY: O reverent fathers of the Spiritual State,
We counsel you be wise and vigilant!
Dame Verity has lighted now of late,
And in her hand bearing the New Testament!

(*The* SPIRITUAL ESTATE *confer in undertones for a moment.*)

BISHOP: I hold it best that we incontinent
Cause hold her fast into captivity,
Unto the third day of the Parliament
And then accuse her of heresy.

(*The* THREE VICES *approach* VERITY.)

FLATTERY: What book is that, harlot, in thy hand?

(*He looks at it.*)

Out! Waylaway! This is the New Testament!
In English tongue, and printed in England!
Heresy, heresy! Fire, fire, incontinent!

VERITY: Forsooth, my friend, you have a wrong judgment,
For in this Book there is no heresy,
But our Christ's word, right douce and redolent—
A springing well of sincere verity!

DECEIT: Come on your way, for all your yellow locks!
Your wanton words but[1] doubt you shall repent!
This night you shall forfare[2] a pair of stocks,
And in the morn be brought to thole judgment.

(VERITY *falls on her knees, not to the* VICES *but to Heaven.*)

VERITY: Get up, thou sleepest all too long, O Lord,
And make some reasonable reformation
Of them that do tramp down Thy gracious Word,
And have a deadly indignation
At them who make the true narration!

FLATTERY: Sit down and take your rest
All night till it be day!

(*They put* VERITY *in the stocks, and return to* SPIRITUALITY.)

[1] without   [2] endure

DECEIT:	My lord, we have with diligence,
	Buckled up well yon blethering bard!
BISHOP:	I think you deserve good recompense.
	Take these ten crowns for your reward!

(CHASTITY *enters intoning to herself a Latin hymn.*)

CHASTITY:	How long shall this inconstant world endure
	That I should banished be so long, alas!
	Few creatures, or none, take of me cure,
	Which makes me many a night lie harbourless!
DILIGENCE:	Lady, I pray you show to me your name!
CHASTITY:	Dame Chastity, banished without a home!
DILIGENCE:	Then pass to ladies of religion,
	Who make their vows to observe chastity.
	Lo, where there sits a Prioress of renown
	Among the rest of Spirituality.

(DILIGENCE *points out the* PRIORESS, *who is one of the members of the* SPIRITUAL ESTATE.)

CHASTITY:	I grant yon lady has vowèd chastity,
	For her profession thereto should accord.
	She made that vow for an abbacy,
	But not for Jesus Christ our Lord . . .
	I shall observe your counsel if I may;
	Come on, and hear what yon lady will say.

(DILIGENCE *and* CHASTITY *approach the* PRIORESS.)

My prudent, lusty Lady Prioress,
Remember how you did vow chastity;
Madame, I pray you of your gentleness
That you would please to have of me pity
And this one night give me harboury!

PRIORESS:	Pass hence, Madame, by Christ you come not here!
	You are contrair to my complexion!
	Go seek lodging from some old monk or friar,
	Perchance they will be your protection.
	Or to prelates make your progression
	Who are obliged to you as well as I!
	Dame Sensual has given direction
	You to exclude out of my company!

(CHASTITY *now addresses the* CHURCHMEN.)

CHASTITY: Lords, I have passed through many uncouth shire,
But in this land I can get no lodging!
Of my name if you would have knowledging
Forsooth, my lords, they call me Chastity.
I you beseech of your graces benign,
Give me lodging this night for charity.

BISHOP: Pass on, Madame, we know you not!
Or by Him that the world has wrought,
Your coming shall be right dear bought,
 If you make longer tarry!

ABBOT: But Doubt we will both live and die
 With our love Sensuality;
We will have no more deal with thee
 Than with the Queen of Fairy.

PARSON: Pass home among the Nuns and dwell,
 Who are of chastity the well—
I trust they will with book and bell
 Receive you in their cloister!

CHASTITY: Sir, when I was the Nuns among,
Out of their dorter they me dang[1]
And would not let me bide so long
 As say my Paternoster.
I see no grace therefore to get.
I hold it best, ere it be late,
For to go prove the temporal state
 If they will me receive.
(CHASTITY *crosses to the* TEMPORAL ESTATE.)
Good day, my lord Temporality,
And you, Merchant of gravity;
Full fain would I have harboury,
 To lodge among the lave.[2]

LORD: Forsooth, we would be well content
To harbour you with good intent,
Were it not we have impediment—
 For why? We two are married!

MERCHANT: But wist our wives that you were here,
They would make all this town in stir,
Therefore we rede you, run arear,
 In dread you be miscarried!
(CHASTITY *now goes to the end of the stage where the*
COMMON PEOPLE *are watching. She approaches*
SOUTAR *and* TAILOR, *near whom are* SOUTAR'S
WIFE *and* TAILOR'S WIFE. *A Soutar is a shoemaker*.)

[1] beat [2] rest

CHASTITY: You men of craft and great ingyne,[1]
Give me harboury for Christ his pine,
And win God's benison, and mine,
And help my hungry heart!

SOUTAR: Is this fair Lady Chastity?

TAILOR: Now welcome by the Trinity!
I think it were a great pity
That thou should lie thereout!

SOUTAR: Sit down, Madame, and take a drink,
And let no sorrow in you sink,
But let us play cap-out.

(*They entertain* CHASTITY.)

SOUTAR'S WIFE: What does the Soutar, my goodman?

TAILOR'S WIFE: Marry, fills the cup and tooms[2] the can
With a young maiden clad in white,
In whom the lurdan takes delight—
I trust, if I can reckon right,
She shapes to lodge with him all night!
Ere he come home, by God I trow
He will be drunken like a sow!

SOUTAR'S WIFE: This is a great despite, I think,
For to receive such a cow-clink!
What is your counsel that we do?

TAILOR'S WIFE: Gossip, this is my counsel, lo!
Ding[3] you the one and I the other

SOUTAR'S WIFE: I am content, by God His Mother!
I think for me these whoreson smaiks[4]
Deserve right well to get their paiks!

(*They drive* CHASTITY *away.*)

TAILOR'S WIFE: Go hence, harlot, how durst thou be so bold
To lodge with our goodmen without licence?
I make a vow by Him that Judas sold,
This rock[5] of mine shall be thy recompense!

SOUTAR'S WIFE: Show me thy name, duddron,[6] with diligence!

CHASTITY: Marry, Chastity is my name, by Saint Blaise.
[1] ability   [2] empties   [3] strike   [4] wretches   [5] distaff   [6] slut

SOUTAR'S WIFE: I pray God may He work on thee vengeance
For I lovèd ne'er chastity all my days!

(She pursues CHASTITY *with her distaff, then the* WIVES *turn on their husbands.)*

SOUTAR'S WIFE: I make a vow to Saint Crispin
I'll be revenged on that graceless groom.
And to begin the play, take there a flap!

(She strikes the SOUTAR.)

SOUTAR: The fiend receive the hands that gave me that!

SOUTAR'S WIFE: What now, whoreson, begins thou now to ban?[1]
Take there another upon thy peeled harn-pan![2]

(to TAILOR'S WIFE*)* What now, gossip, wilt thou not
take my part?

TAILOR'S WIFE: That shall I do, gossip, with all my heart.

(As the WIVES *chase their husbands off,* SOLACE *catches sight of* CHASTITY *and speaks to the* KING.)

SOLACE: Sovereign, get up and see a heavenly sight,
A fair lady in white habilament!
She may be peer unto a king or knight,
Most like an angel by my judgment!

(The KING *rises from among the ladies.)*

KING: I shall go see that sight incontinent,
(to SENSUALITY*)* Madame, behold if you have
knowledging
Of yon lady, or what is her intent.
Thereafter we shall turn but[3] tarrying.

SENSUALITY: Sir, let me see what yon matter may mean—
Perchance that I may know her by her face.
(She looks more closely at CHASTITY.)
But doubt, this is Dame Chastity, I ween!
Sir, I and she cannot bide in one place!
But if it be the pleasure of your grace,
That I remain into your company,
This woman right hastily make chase,
That she no more be seen in this country!

KING: As ever you please, sweetheart, so shall it be!
Dispose her as you think expedient.
Even as you list to let her live or die,
I will refer that thing to your judgment.

---

[1] curse   [2] bald cranium   [3] without

SENSUALITY: I will that she be banishèd incontinent,
               And never to come again in this country;
               And if she does, but doubt she shall repent,
               Also perchance a doleful death shall die!
               Pass on, Sir Sapience and Discretion,
               And banish her out of the King's presence!

DECEIT: That shall we do, Madame, by God's passion!
               We shall do thy command with diligence.
               And at your hands deserve good recompense.
               Dame Chastity, come on, be not aghast!
               We shall right soon upon your own expense
               Into the stocks your bonny foot make fast!

               (*The* VICES *place* CHASTITY *in the stocks beside*
               VERITY.)

CHASTITY: Sister, alas, this is a care-full case,
               That we with princes should be so abhorred!

VERITY: Be blithe, sister, I trust within short space,
               That we shall be right honourably restored,
               And with the King we shall be at concord,
               For I heard tell Divine Correction
               Is new landed, thanks be to Christ our Lord!
               I wot he will be our protection!

               (*A fanfare. Enter* CORRECTION'S VARLET.)

VARLET: Sirs, stand back and hold you coy.[1]
               I am the King Correction's boy,
                   Come here to dress his place!
               See that you make obedience
               Unto his noble excellence
                   From time you see his face!
               He has made reformations
               Out-through all Christian nations,
                   Where he finds great debates.
               And so far as I understand,
               He shall reform into this land
                   Even all the Three Estates.
               For silence I protest
                   Both of Lord, Laird and Lady!
               Now will I run but rest
                   And tell that all is ready!

               (*Another fanfare. Exit* CORRECTION'S VARLET.
               The THREE VICES *go into conference.*)
                   [1] quiet

DECEIT: Brother, hear you yon proclamation?
I dread full sore of reformation,
    Yon message makes me mangèd.[1]
What is your counsel, to me tell!
Remain we here, by God himsel',
    We will be all three hangèd!

FLATTERY: I'll gang to Spirituality
And preach out-through his diosee,
    Where I will be unknown,
Or keep me close in some cloister
With many a piteous Paternoster,
    Till all their blasts be blown.

DECEIT: I'll be well treated, as you ken,
With my masters, the Merchant men,
    Who can make small debate;
You know right few of them that thrives
Or can beguile the landward wives
    Without their man Deceit.
Now, Falsehood, what shall be thy shift?

FALSEHOOD: No, care thou not, man, for my thrift!
    Trows thou that I be daft?
No, I will live a lusty life
Withouten any sturt or strife,
    Among the men of craft.

DECEIT: Falsehood, I would we made a bond—
Now, while the King is yet sleepand[2]
    What rack to steal his box?

FALSEHOOD: Now, well said by the Sacrament!
I shall it steal incontinent,
    Though it had twenty locks!

(FALSEHOOD *steals the* KING'S *box.*)

Lo, here the box! Now let us go,
This may suffice for our rewards!

DECEIT: Yea, that it may, man, by this day!
It may well make us landward lairds!
Now let us cast away our clothes,
In dread some follow on the chase!

FALSEHOOD: Right well devised, man, by Saint Blaise,
Would God we were out of this place!

(*Here they cast away their disguises.*)

[1] confounded   [2] sleeping

DECEIT:	Now, since there is no man to wrong us,
	I pray you, brother, with my heart,
	Let us go part this pelf among us,
	Then hastily we shall depart!
FALSEHOOD:	Trows thou to get as much as I?
	That shalt thou not! I stole the box!
	Thou did nothing but lookit by,
	Aye lurking like a wily fox!

(DECEIT *and* FALSEHOOD *fight.*)

FALSEHOOD:	Alas for ever my eye is out!
DECEIT:	Upon thy craig[1] take there a clout!

(FLATTERY *has meantime stolen the box and runs out pursued by* DECEIT *and* FALSEHOOD. *Their flight is hastened by the fanfare and stately march to which enter* DIVINE CORRECTION *and his train.*)

ESTATES	(*sing*): Rex tremendae majestratis,
	Juste judex ultionis,
	Rex omnipotens gloriae.
CORRECTION:	I am callèd Divine Correction.
	Where I am not is no tranquillity!
	By me traitors and tyrants are put down
	Who think no shame of their iniquity.
	What is a King? Nought but an officer,
	To cause his lieges live in equity,
	And under God to be a punisher
	Of trespassers against His Majesty.
	I am a judge, right potent and severe,
	Come to do justice many a thousand mile.
	I am so constant, both in peace and war,
	No bribe or favour may my sight o'er-sile.[2]

(GOOD COUNSEL *enters and runs to greet his master.*)

GOOD COUNSEL:	Welcome, my lord, welcome ten thousand times
	To all the true men of this region!
	Welcome for to correct all faults and crimes
	Among this cankered congregation!
	Loose Chastity, I make supplication,
	Put to freedom fair Lady Verity,
	Who by unfaithful folk of this nation
	Lies bound full fast into captivity!
CORRECTION:	I marvel, Good Counsel, how that may be—
	Are you not with the King familiar?

[1] throat   [2] obscure

D

GOOD COUNSEL: That I am not, my lord, full woe is me,
But like a beggar am holden at the bar.

CORRECTION: Where lie yon ladies in captivity?

(*He turns to* VERITY *and* CHASTITY *in the stocks.*)

How now, sisters, who has you so disguisèd?

VERITY: Unfaithful members of iniquity,
Despitefully, my lord, has us suppressèd.

CORRECTION: Go, put yon ladies to their liberty
Incontinent, and break down all the stocks!
But doubt, they are full dear welcome to me!
Make diligence! Methinks you do but mocks!
Speed hand, and spare not for to break the locks,
And tenderly to take them by the hand!
Had I them here, these knaves should ken my knocks,
That them oppressed and banished from this land!

(*Members of* CORRECTION's *retinue release* VERITY *and* CHASTITY. *The* COURTIERS *spy* CORRECTION.)

WANTONNESS: Solace, knows thou not what I see?
A knight, or else a king thinks me,
Brother, what may this mean?

SOLACE: Whether that he be friend or foe,
Stand still and hear what he will say,
Such one I have not seen!

PLACEBO: I rede us, put upon the King,
And waken him out of his sleeping!

(*He rouses the* KING *from the arms of* SENSUALITY.)

Sir, rise up and see an unco[1] thing!
Get up, you lie too long!

SENSUALITY: Put on your hood, John-fool! You rave!
How dare you be so pert, Sir Knave,
To touch the King? So Christ me save,
False whoreson, thou shalt hang!

(CORRECTION *approaches the* KING.)

CORRECTION: Get up, Sir King, you have sleepèd enough
Into the arms of Lady Sensual!

(*The* KING *rises and faces him.*)

Remember how, into the time of Noë
For the foul stink and sin of lechery,

[1] strange

God by my wand did all the world destroy.
Sodom and Gommorra right so full rigorously
For that vile sin were burnt most cruelly.
Therefore I thee command incontinent
Banish from thee that whore Sensuality
Or beyond doubt rudely thou shalt repent!

KING:

By whom have you so great authority?
Who does presume for to correct a King?
Know you not me, great King Humanity,
That in my region royally does reign?

CORRECTION:

I have power great princes to down-thring[1]
That live contrair the Majesty Divine,
Against the truth who plainly do malign;
Repent they not, I put them to ruin!
I will begin at thee, who art the head,
And make on thee the first reformation,
Thy lieges then will follow thee indeed!
Swift, harlot, hence without dilation![2]

SENSUALITY:

My lord, I make you supplication,
Give me licence to pass again to Rome!
Among the princes of that nation,
I let you know my fresh beauty will bloom!
Adieu, Sir King, I may no longer tarry!
Not that I care, as good love comes as goes!
I recommend you to the Queen of Faerie—
I see you will be guided by my foes!

(SENSUALITY *and her retinue pass to the* ESTATE
SPIRITUAL.)

My lordës of the Spiritual State,
Venus preserve you air[3] and late!
For I can make no more debate,
      I am parted with your king,
And am banishèd this region,
By council of Correction.
Be ye not my protection,
      I may seek my lodging!

BISHOP:

Welcome, our days' darling!
Welcome with all our heart!
We without feigning
Shall plainly take your part!

[1] overthrow   [2] delay   [3] early

(SENSUALITY, HOMELINESS, DANGER *take their places with* BISHOP, ABBOT *and* PARSON. CORRECTION *returns to the* KING.)

CORRECTION:
Since you are quit of Sensuality,
Receive into your service Good Counsel,
And right so this fair Lady Chastity,
Till you marry some Queen of blood royal.
Observe then chastity matrimonial.
Right so receive Verity by the hand . . .
Use their counsel, your fame shall never fall;
With them, therefore, make a perpetual bond!

(*The* KING *receives* GOOD COUNSEL, CHASTITY *and* VERITY.)

Now, sir, attend to what I say,
Observe that same both night and day,
And never let them part you frae,[1]
        Or else without a doubt,
Turn you to Sensuality,
To vicious life and ribaldry,
Out of your realm right shamefully,
        You shall be rooted out!

KING:
I am content to your counsel t'incline.
At your command shall be all that is mine.

(*Solemn music. He embraces* CORRECTION.)

CORRECTION:
I counsel you incontinent
To cause proclaim a Parliament
        Of all the Three Estates,
That they be here with diligence
To make to you obedience
        And then dress all debates!

KING:
That shall be done, but[2] more demand.
Ho, Diligence, come here from hand
        And take your information.
Go, warn the Spirituality,
Right so the Temporality,
        By open proclamation,
In goodly haste for to appear
In their most honourable manner
        To give us their counsels!
Who that is absent, to them show
That they shall under-lie the Law
        And punished be that fails!

        [1] from   [2] without

DILIGENCE: Sir, I shall both in borough and land,
              With diligence do your command,
                  Upon my own expense.
              Sir, I have served you all this year,
              But I got never one dinner
                  Yet for my recompense!

KING: Pass on, and thou shalt be regarded
              And for they service well rewarded,
                  For why? With my consent,
              Thou shalt have yearly for thy hire
              The tithe mussels of the Ferry-mire
                  Confirmed in Parliament.

DILIGENCE: I will get riches through that rent
                  After the days of Doom,
              When in the coal-pits of Tranent
                  Butter will grow on broom!
              All night I had so great a drouth, [1]
                  I might not sleep a wink,
              Ere I proclaim aught with my mouth,
                  But doubt I must have drink!

              (*While* DILIGENCE *refreshes himself* DIVINE CORREC-
              TION *tackles the* COURTIERS.)

CORRECTION: Come here, Placebo and Solace,
              With your companion Wantonness,
                  I know well your condition.
              For enticing King Humanity
              To receive Sensuality
                  You must suffer punition!

WANTONNESS: We grant, my Lord, we have done ill;
              Therefore we put us in your will,
                  But we have been abused!

PLACEBO: For in good faith, sir, we believed
              That lechery had no man grieved
                  Because it was so used!

SOLACE: Sir, we shall mend our condition
              So you give us remission . . .
                  But give us leave to sing,
              To dance, to play at chess and tables,
              To read stories and merry fables
                  For pleasure of our King!
                        [1] thirst

CORRECTION:
See that you do no other crime!
You shall be pardoned at this time;
    For why? As I suppose,
Princes may sometimes seek solace
With mirth and lawful merriness,
    Their spirits to rejoice.
And right so hawking and hunting
Are honest pastimes for a king,
    Into the time of peace;
And learn to run a heavy spear,
That he into the time of war
    May follow at the chase!

KING:
Where is Sapience and Discretion?
And why comes not Devotion near?

VERITY:
They three were Flattery and Deceit,
And Falsehood, that unhappy loon,
Against us three that made debate,
And banished us from town to town.

CHASTITY:
They made us two fall in a swoon,
When they us lockèd in the stocks.
That dastard knave, Discretion,
Full thefteously did steal your box!

KING:
The Devil take them, since they are gone!
I make a vow to sweet Saint Fillan,
When I them find they'll bear their paiks,[1]
I see they have playèd me the glaiks![2]
Good Counsel, now show me the best,
How I shall keep my realm in rest.

GOOD COUNSEL:
The principal point, sir, of a king's office,
Is for to do to every man justice,
And for to mix his justice with mercy,
Without rigour, favour or partiality.
Who guide them well, they win immortal fame;
Who the countrair, they get perpetual shame.
The Chronicles to know, I you exhort;
There shall you find both good and evil report;
For every prince, after his quality,
Though he be dead, his deeds shall never die!
Sir, if you please for to use my counsel,
Your fame and name shall be perpetual.

(*A fanfare*).

    [1] punishment   [2] deception

DILIGENCE:

Hoyez, hoyez, hoyez!
At the command of King Humanity
I warn and charge all members of Parliament,
Both Spiritual State and Temporality,
That to his grace they be obedient
And speed them to the court, incontinent,
In good order, arrayèd royally.
Who is absent or inobedient,
The King's pleasure they shall under-lie!

(*To the audience.*)

Also I make you exhortation,
Since you have heard the first part of our play,
Go, take a drink, and make collation;
Each man drink to his marrow, I you pray.
Tarry not long, it is late in the day.
Let some drink ale, and some drink claret wine;
By great doctors of physic I hear say
That mighty drink comforts the dull ingyne![1]

(*Music, a march. All go off.*)

[1] intellect

THE END OF THE FIRST PART

SECOND PART

Fanfare. DILIGENCE *comes on to the empty stage as if to make a proclamation. Before he can do so, the* POOR MAN *enters, addressing the audience.*

POOR MAN:
Of your alms, good folk, for God's love of heaven,
For I have motherless bairns either six or seven!
If you'll give me no good, for the love of Jesus,
Show me the right way to St. Andrews.

DILIGENCE:
Where have we gotten this goodly companion?
Swift! Forth of the field, thou false, ragged loon!
Officers, come chase this carl away,
Or deil a word you'll get more of our play!

(*The* POOR MAN *climbs on to the* KING'S *throne.*)

Come down, or by God's crown, false loon I shall
slay thee!

POOR MAN:
Now swear by thy burnt shins, the devil ding[1] them
from you!

DILIGENCE:
Quick, beggar bogle, haste thee away,
Thou art over pert to spoil our play!

POOR MAN:
I will give for your play not a sow's fart
For there is right little play at my hungry heart!

DILIGENCE:
What devil ails this crooked carl?

POOR MAN:
Marry, meikle sorrow!
I cannot get, though I gasp, to beg not or borrow.

DILIGENCE:
Where dwells thou, bankrupt, or what is thine
intent?

POOR MAN:
I dwell into Lothian, a mile from Tranent.

DILIGENCE:
Where would thou be, carl? The sooth to me show!

POOR MAN:
Sir, even to St. Andrews, for to seek law.

DILIGENCE:
For to seek law, in Edinburgh is the nearest way.

[1] strike

POOR MAN: Sir, I sought law there this many a dear day;
               But I could get none at Session or Senate,
               Therefore the meikle dumb devil drown all that
                    menyie![1]

DILIGENCE: Show me thy matter, man, with all the circum-
                    stance,
               How thou has happenèd on this unhappy chance.

POOR MAN: Good man, will you give me of your charity
               And I shall declare you the black verity?
               My father was an old man with grey hair
               And was of age four score of years and more,
               And Maud my mother was four score and fifteen;
               And with my labour I did them both sustain.
               We had a mare that carried salt and coal,
               And every year she brought us home a foal.
               We had three kye[2] that were both fat and fair,
               None tidier hence to the town of Ayr.
               My father was so weak of blood and bone,
               That he died, wherefore my mother made great
                    moan,
               Then she died within a day or two,
               And there began my poverty and woe.
               Our good grey mare was grazing on the field
               And our land's laird took her for his hire-yield[3].
               Our vicar took the best cow by the head
               Incontinent, when my father was dead.
               And when the vicar heard tell how that my mother
               Was dead, from hand he took from me another.
               Then Meg my wife did mourn both even and
                    morrow
               Till at the last she died for very sorrow.
               And when the vicar heard tell my wife was dead,
               The third cow he cleekèd[4] by the head.
               Their hindmost clothes, that were of rapploch[5]
                    grey,
               The vicar made his clerk bear them away.
               When all was gone I might make no debate,
               But with my bairns passed for to beg my meat.
               Now I have told you the black verity
               How I am brought into this misery.

DILIGENCE: How did the Parson? Was he not thy good friend?

POOR MAN: The devil stick him, he cursed me for my teind[6]
               And holds me yet under that same process

[1] pack   [2] cattle   [3] a fine   [4] caught   [5] coarse cloth   [6] tithe

That caused me lack the Sacrament at Pace.[1]
In good faith, sir, though you would cut my throat,
I have no gear except one English groat
Which I propose to give a man of law.

DILIGENCE: Thou art the daftest fool that ever I saw!
Trows thou, man, by the law, to get remede
Of men of Church? No, never till thou be dead!
Be sure of priests thou wilt get no support.

POOR MAN: If that be true, the fiend receive the sort!
So, since I see I get no other grace,
I will lie down and rest me in this place.

(*He does so. Enter* PARDONER, *who is* FLATTERY *in
his disguise.*)

PARDONER: Bona dies, bona dies!
Devout people, good day I say you,
Now tarry a little while I pray you
    Till I be with you known!
Wot you well how I am named?
A noble man and undefamed,
    If all the sooth were shown.
I am Sir Robert Rome-raker,
A perfect public pardoner
    Admitted by the Pope.
Sirs, I shall show you, for my wage,
My pardons and my pilgrimage,
    Which you shall see and grope.
I give to the devil with good intent
This woeful wicked New Testament,
    With them that it translated.
Since laymen knew the verity,
Pardoners get no charity
    Without that they debate it.
Deil fell the brain that has it wrought,
So fall them that the Book home brought,
    Also I pray to the Rood
That Martin Luther, that false loon,
Black Bullenger and Melancthon
    Had been smoored in their cude.[2]
By Him that bare the crown of thorn
I would Saint Paul had never been born,
    Also I would his books
Were never read into the Kirk

---

[1] Easter   [2] smothered in their baptismal gown

But among friars into the mirk[1]
    Or riven among the rooks!
My patent pardons you may see
Come from the Khan of Tartary
    Well sealed with oyster shells.
Though you have no contrition
You shall have full remission
    With help of books and bells.
Here is a relic, long and broad,
Of Finn MacColl[2] the right jaw blade
    With teeth and all together.
Of Colin's cow here is a horn
For eating of MacConnel's corn
    Was slain into Balquhidder.
Here is a cord both great and long,
Which hangèd Johnnie the Armstrong,
    Of good hemp soft and sound.
Good holy people, I stand for'ard,
Whoever is hangèd with this cord
    Needs never to be drowned!
Come win the pardon, now let see,
For meal, for malt or for money,
    For cock, hen, goose, or grice![3]
Of relics here I have a hunder.
Why come you not? This is a wonder.
    I trow you be not wise!

(*The* POOR MAN *wakes up.*)

POOR MAN: What thing was yon that I heard crack and cry?
I have been dreaming and drivelling of my kye!
With my right hand my whole body I sain,[4]
Saint Bride, Saint Bride, send me my kye again!
(*He sees the* PARDONER.)
I see standing yonder a holy man;
To make me help, let me see if I can!

PARDONER: Come win the pardon, and then I shall thee sain!

POOR MAN: Will that pardon get me my kye again?

PARDONER: Carl, of thy kye I have nothing ado.
Come win my pardon, and kiss my relics too.

(*He blesses him with his relics.*)

Now loose thy purse, and lay down thy offering,
And thou shalt have my pardon even from hand.
Now win the pardon, limmer,[5] or thou art lost!
[1] dark   [2] a giant   [3] pig   [4] bless   [5] rascal

POOR MAN: My holy father, what will that pardon cost?

PARDONER: Let see what money thou bearest in thy bag.

POOR MAN: I have but one groat here bound into a rag.

PARDONER: Hast thou no other money but one groat?

POOR MAN: If I have more, sir, come and ripe my coat!

PARDONER: Give me that groat, man, if thou hast no more.

POOR MAN: With all my heart, master, lo, take it, there!
Now let me see your pardon, with your leave.

PARDONER: A thousand year of pardons I thee give!

POOR MAN: A thousand year? I will not live so long.
Deliver me it, master, and let me gang!

PARDONER: A thousand year I lay upon thy head,
With *totiens quotiens*; now no longer plead.
Thou hast received thy pardon now already.

POOR MAN: But I can see nothing, sir, by our Lady!

PARDONER: What craves the carl? Methinks thou art not wise!

POOR MAN: I crave my groat, or else my merchandise!

PARDONER: I gave thee pardon for a thousand year!

POOR MAN: How shall I get that pardon? Let me hear!

PARDONER: Stand still, and I shall tell thee the whole story!
When thou art dead and gone to Purgatory,
Being condemned to pain a thousand year,
Then shall thy pardon thee relieve but weir![1]
Now be content! You are a marvellous man!

POOR MAN: Shall I get nothing for my groat till then?

PARDONER: That shalt thou not! I make it to you plain!

(*The poor man is now very angry.*)

POOR MAN: No? Then, gossip, give me my groat again!
What say you, master? Call you this good reason,
That he should promise me a good pardon,
And here receive my money in this stead,
Then make to me no payment till I be dead?
When I am dead, I know full certainly

[1] without doubt

My silly soul will pass to Purgatory.
Declare me this! Now God nor Belial bind thee,
When I am there, curst carl, where shall I find thee?
Not into heaven, but rather into hell!
When thou art there, thou cannot help thysel'!

PARDONER: Swift! Stand aback! I trow this man be mangit![1]
Thou gets not this groat, though thou should be
    hangèd!

POOR MAN: Give me my groat, well bound into my clout!
Or by God's bread, Robin shall bear a rout!

(*He sets upon the* PARDONER *and chases him off.*)

DILIGENCE: What kind of fooling is this all day?
Swift, smaiks,[2] out of the field, away!
Into a prison put them soon
Then hang then when the play is done!

(*A fanfare and a march. Enter the* KING, *his*
COURTIERS, DIVINE CORRECTION, *the* VIRTUES. *The
music continues with the speech.*)

Famous people, attend, and you shall see
The Three Estates of this nation,
Come to the court with a strange gravity.
Therefore I make you supplication
Till you have heard our whole narration
To keep silence and be patient I pray you.
Howbeit we speak by adulation
We shall say nothing but the truth, I say you!

(THE THREE ESTATES *enter, led by their* VICES.
They are walking backwards, SPIRITUALITY *led by*
FLATTERY, TEMPORALITY *by* DECEIT, *and* BURGESSES
by FALSEHOOD.)

WANTONNESS: Now, broad benedicite!
What thing is yon that I see?
    Look, Solace, my heart!

SOLACE: Brother Wantonness, what thinks thou?
Yon are the Three Estates, I trow,
Going backwards!

WANTONNESS: Backwards? Backwards? Out! Waylaway!
It is a great shame for them, I say,
    Backward to gang.
I trow the King Correction

---

[1] deranged   [2] wretches

Must make a reformation,
　　Ere it be long!
Now let us go and tell the King!
Sir, we have seen a marvellous thing,
　　By our judgment!
The Three Estates of this region,
Are coming backwards, through this town,
　　To the Parliament!

KING:　　Backward, backward, how may that be?
Make speed them hastily to me,
　　In dread that they go wrong!

PLACEBO:　　Sir, I see them yonder coming,
They will be here even from hand,
　　As fast as they may gang!

GOOD COUNSEL:　　Sir, hold you still and scare them not,
Till you perceive what be their thought,
　　And see what men them lead.
And let the King Correction
Make a sharp inquisition,
　　And mark them by the heads!
(THE ESTATES *are singing a chorus made up from words from the following verses:*)

SPIRITUALITY:　　Gloire, honour, laud, triumph and victory,
Be to your mighty prudent excellence;
Here are we come, all the Estates Three,
Ready to make our due obedience,
At your command with humble observance,
As may pertain to Spirituality,
With counsel of the Temporality.

TEMPORALITY:　　Sir, you with mighty courage at command
Of your super-excellent Majesty,
Shall make service, both with our heart and hand,
And shall not dread in thy defence to die;
We are content, but doubt, that we may see
That noble, heavenly King Correction,
So he with mercy make punition.

BURGESSES:　　Sir, we are here your Burgesses and Merchants.
Thanks be to God that we may see your face,
Trusting we may now into divers lands
Convoy our gear with support of your grace;
For now, I trust, we shall get rest and peace,
When mis-doers are with your sword o'er-thrown,
Then may loyal merchants live upon their own.
(*The singing ends.*)

KING:　　Welcome to me, my prudent lordës all,

You are my members, suppose I be your head:
Sit down that we may with your just counsel
Against mis-doers find sovereign remede.

CORRECTION: My tender friends, I pray you with my heart,
Declare to me the thing that I would speir.[1]
What is the cause that you go all backward?
The verity thereof fain would I hear.

BISHOP: Sovereign, we have gone so this many a year.
Howbeit you think we go undecently,
We think we go right wonder pleasantly.

DILIGENCE: Sit down, my lords, into your proper places:
Then let the King consider all such cases.
Sit down, Sir Scribe, and sit down Deemster, too
And fence the Court as you were wont to do.

(*Music* as THE ESTATES *take their places and all
present dispose themselves for a court of enquiry.*)

KING: My prudent lordës of the Three Estates,
It is our will, above all other thing,
For to reform all those who make debates
Contrair the right, who daily do malign,
And they that do the Common-Weal down-thring.[2]
With help and counsel of King Correction,
It is our will for to make punishing,
And plain oppressors put to subjection.

BISHOP: What thing is this, sir, that you have devised?
Sirs, you have need for to be well advised.
Be not hasty into your execution,
And be not o'er extreme in your punition.
And if you please to do, sir, as we say,
Postpone this Parliament to another day.
For why? The people of this region
Will not endure extreme correction!

CORRECTION: Is this the part, my lords, that you will take
To make us supportation to correct?
It does appear that you are culpable,
That are not to correction applicable!
Swift, Diligence, go show it is our will,
That every man oppressed give in his bill.

DILIGENCE (*proclaims*): It is the King Correction's will
That every man oppressed give in his bill.

(JOHN THE COMMON-WEAL, *a sturdy figure in rags,
rushes in.*)

[1] ask   [2] overthrow

JOHN: Out of my way! For God's sake let me go!
            Tell me again, good master, what you say.

DILIGENCE: I warn all that be wrongeously offended,
            Come and complain and they shall be amended.
            What is thy name, fellow? That would I feel.

JOHN: Forsooth, they call me John the Common-Weal.
            Good master, I would ask at you one thing—
            Where trust you I shall find yon new-made King?

DILIGENCE: Come over, and I shall show thee to his grace.

            (*He leads* JOHN *to the* KING.)

JOHN: God's benison light in that lucky face!

KING: Show me thy name, good man, I thee command.

JOHN: Marry, John the Common-Weal of fair Scotland.

            (*The* KING *surveys* JOHN'S *rags,*)

KING: The Common-Weal has been among his foes.

JOHN: Yes, sir, that makes the Common-Weal want
            clothes!

KING: What is the cause the Common-Weal is crookèd?

JOHN: Because the Common-Weal has been o'er lookèd.

KING: What makes thee look so with a dreary heart?

JOHN: Because the Three Estates go all backward.

KING: Sir Common-Weal, know you the limmers that
            them lead?

JOHN: Their canker colours, I know them by the heads!
            As for our reverend fathers of Spirituality,
            They are led by Flattery and careless Sensuality,
            And as you see, Temporality has need of correction,
            Who has long time been led by public oppression.
            Lo, here is Falsehood, and Deceit well I ken,
            Leaders of the Merchants and silly craftsmen.
            What marvel though the Three Estates backward
                gang,
            When such a vile company dwells them among,
            Which has ruled this rout many dear days,
            Which makes John the Common-Weal lack his
                warm clothes?
            Thou feignèd Flattery, the fiend fart in thy face!
            When you were guider of the court we got little grace!

My sovereign Lord Correction, I make you suppli-
> cation,
Put these tried trickers from Christ's congregation!

CORRECTION: As you have devised, but doubt it shall be done!
Come here, my sergeants, and do your debt soon!
Put these three robbers into prison strong,
Howbeit you should hang them, you do them no
> wrong!

FIRST SERGEANT: Sovereign lord, we shall obey your commands.
Brother, upon these scoundrels lay on your hands!

SECOND SERGT.: Come here, gossip, come here, come here!
Your reckless life you shall repent.
When were you wont to be so sweir?[1]
Stand still and be obedient!

(*The* SERGEANTS *hustle the* THREE VICES *to the stocks.*)

Put in your legs into the stocks,
For you had never meeter hose!
These stewats stink as they were brocks!
Now are you siccar,[2] I suppose!

(*They go to* CORRECTION.)

My lord, we have done your commands.
Shall we put the ladies in captivity?

CORRECTION: Yea, hardly lay on them your hands!
Right so upon Sensuality.

(SENSUALITY *turns to the* BISHOP.)

SENSUALITY: Adieu, my lord!

BISHOP: Adieu, my own sweet heart!
Now grief fall me that we two must part!

SENSUALITY: My lord, howbeit this parting does me pain,

(THE SERGEANTS *chase* SENSUALITY *and her retinue
away to a place among the* POOR PEOPLE *at the foot
of the stage.*)

LORD: My lords, you know the Three Estates,
For Common-Weal should make debates.
Let now among us be devised
Such acts as by good men be praised;
And for to save us from murmell,[3]
Soon, Diligence, fetch us Good Counsel!
For why? He is a man that knows
Both the Canon and the Civil Laws.

(DILIGENCE *passes to* GOOD COUNSEL.)

[1] lazy   [2] sure   [3] complaint

E

DILIGENCE:
Father, you must incontinent
Pass to the Lords of Parliament;
For why? They are determined all
To do nothing without counsel.

GOOD COUNSEL:
My lords, God glad the company!
What is the cause you send for me?

MERCHANT:
Sit down and give us your counsel,
How we shall slaik[1] the great murmell
Of poor people, that is well known
And as the Common-Weal has shown.
And as we know it is the King's will
That good remede be put there till,
Sir Common-Weal, keep you the bar,
Let none except yourself come near!

(JOHN *lays his hand on the* POOR MAN.)

JOHN:
You must let this poor creature
Support me for to keep the door.
I know his name full certainly,
He will complain as well as I.

GOOD COUNSEL:
My worthy lords, since you have ta'en on hand
Some reformation to make into this land,
And as you know it is the King his mind
Who to the Common-Weal has aye been kind,
Though reive[2] and theft be stanched well enough,
Yet something more belongeth to the plough.
Now into peace you should provide for wars
And be sure of how many thousand spears
The King may be when he has ought to do;
For why, my lords, this is my reason, lo!
The husbandmen and commons they were wont
Go into battle foremost in the front.
But I have lost all my experience
Without you make some better diligence—
The Common-Weal must otherwise be styled
Or by my faith the King will be beguiled!
The poor commons daily as you may see
Decline down to extreme poverty
And are destroyed without God on them rue!

POOR MAN:
Sir, by God's bread, that tale is very true!
It is well known I had both neat and horse,
Now all my gear you see upon my corse.

[1] abate   [2] pillage

CORRECTION: Ere I depart I think to make an order!

JOHN: I pray you, sir, begin first at the Border,
               For how can we fend us against England,
               When we can not, within our native land,
               Destroy our own Scots, common traitor thieves,
               Who to loyal labourers daily do mischief?
               Were I a king, my lord, by God his wounds,
               Who'er held common thieves within their bounds,
               Where through that daily loyal men might be
                   wronged,
               Without remede these chieftains should be hanged!

LORD: What other enemies hast thou let us ken?

JOHN: Sir, I complain upon the idle men.
               For why, sir, it is God's own bidding
               All Christian men to work for their living.
               This is against the strong beggars,
               Fiddlers, pipers and pardoners,
               These jugglers, jesters and idle coutchers,[1]
               These carriers and these quintessencers,
               These bauble-bearers and these bards,
               These sweir swingeours[2] with lords and lairds.
               This is against these great fat friars,
               Augustines, Carmelites and Cordelers,
               And all others that in cowls are clad,
               Who labour not and are well fed—
               I mean, not labouring spiritually,
               Nor for their living corporally.
               Lying in dens like idle dogs,
               I them compare to well fed hogs!
               I think they do themselves abuse,
               Seeing that they the world refuse;
               Having professed such poverty,
               Then fly fast from necessity!

CORRECTION: Whom upon more will you complain?

JOHN: Marry, on more and more again!
               For the poor man who with care cries
               At the misuse of Law's assize.
               A petty picking thief is hanged,
               But he that all the world has wronged—
               A cruel tyrant, a strong transgressor,
               A common public plain oppressor—
               By bribes may he obtain favours

                   [1] gamblers   [2] idle rascals

Of treasures and compositors,
And through laws, consistorial,
Prolix, corrupt and perpetual,
The common people are so put under,
Though they be poor, it is no wonder!

CORRECTION: Good John, I grant all that is true;
Your misfortune full sore I rue!
So, my lord Temporality,
I you command in time that ye
Expel oppression off your lands.
Also I say to you merchants,
If ever I find, by land or sea,
Deceit into your company,
Which is to Common-weal contrair,
I vow to God I shall not spare!
My lords, what say you to this play?

LORD: My sovereign lords, we will obey,
And take your part with heart and hand,
Whatever you please us to command.
But we beseech you, sovereign,
Of all our crimes that are by-gone,
To give us a remission,
And here we make to you condition
The Common-Weal for to defend,
From henceforth to our lives end!

CORRECTION: On that condition I am content
To pardon you since you repent—
The Common-Weal take by the hand
And make with him perpetual band!
(*The* LORDS *and the* BURGESSES *receive* JOHN THE
COMMON-WEAL.)
John, have you any more debates
Against my lords, the Spiritual Estates?

JOHN: No, sir, I dare not speak the sooth—
Who plains on priests gets little ruth!

CORRECTION: Flyte[1] on they foe, fool, I desire thee,
So that you show but the verity!

JOHN: Gramercy, then I shall not spare,
First to complain on our vicar.
The poor cottar being like to die,
Having small infants two or three,
And has two kye[2] withouten more,

                    [1] rage   [2] cattle

The vicar must have one of them,
With the grey coat that haps[1] the bed,
Howbeit the wife be poorly clad!
And if the wife die on the morn,
Though all the bairns should be forlorn,
The other cow he cleeks[2] away,
With the poor coat of raploch grey.
Would God this custom were put down,
Which was never founded by reason!

LORD: Are all these tales true that thou tells?

POOR MAN: True, sir, the devil stick me else!
For by the Holy Trinity,
The same was practisèd on me!

(JOHN *singles out the* PARSON.)

JOHN: Our parson here he takes no other pyne
But to receive his teinds and spend them syne![3]

POOR MAN: Our bishops with their surplices of white,
They flow in riches royally and delight;
Like paradise are their palaces and places,
And lack no pleasure of the fairest faces!
No doubt I would think it a pleasant life
Aye when I list to part me from my wife
They take another of far greater beauty.
But ever alas, my lords, that may not be,
For I am bound, alas, in marriage,
But they like rams run rudely in their rage!

PARSON: Thou lies, false whoreson ragged loon!
There are no priests in all this town
That ever used such vicious crafts!

BISHOP (*to* TEMPORALITY): My lords, why do you thole[4]
that lurdan loon
Of Churchmen to speak such detraction?
Yon villain puts me out of charity!

LORD: Why, my lord, say she aught but verity?
You cannot stop a poor man for to plain!

BISHOP: I will not suffer such words of yon villain!

POOR MAN: Then make give me my three fat kye again!

BISHOP: False carl, to speak to me stands thou not awe?

[1] covers   [2] catches   [3] then   [4] suffer

POOR MAN: The fiend receive them that first devised that law!
                Within an hour after my dad was dead
                The vicar had my cow hard by the head!

PARSON: False whoreson carl, I say that law is good,
                Because it has been long our consuetude!

POOR MAN: When I am Pope, that law I shall put down!
                It is a sore law for the poor common!

BISHOP: I make a vow these words thou shalt repent!

GOOD COUNSEL: I you require, my lords, be patient!
                We came not here for disputations:
                We came to make good reformations!

MERCHANT: My lords, conclude that all the temporal lands
                Be set in feu to labourers with their hands,
                With restrictions as shall be devised,
                That they may live and not to be suppressed,
                And when the King does make him for the war,
                Let them be ready with harness, bow and spear!
                And for myself, my lord, this I conclude.

GOOD COUNSEL: So say we all, your reason is so good!

JOHN: What do ye of the corpse-present and the cow?

BISHOP: We will want nothing that we have in use,
                Kirtle nor cow, teind[1] lamb, teind grice[2] nor goose!

LORD: We shall decree here that the King his grace
                Shall write unto the Pope his Holiness.
                With his consent, by proclamation,
                Both corpse-present and cow we shall cry down!

BISHOP: To that, my lords, we plainly disassent!
                Note that thereof I take an instrument!

LORD: My lord, by Him that all the world has wrought,
                We care not whether you consent or not!
                You are but one estate and we are two!
                Et ubi maior pars ibi tota!

JOHN: My lords, you have right prudently concluded!
                Attend now how the land is clean denuded
                Of gold and silver that daily goes to Rome,
                For bribes, more that the rest of Christendom.
                Never a penny should go to Rome at all,
                No more than did to Peter or to Paul!

                        [1] tithe   [2] pig

MERCHANT: We merchants, well I wot, within our bounds
  Have furnished priests ten hundred thousand
    pounds
  For their finance; none knows as well as we!
  Therefore, my lords, devise some remedy!
  Sir Simony has made with them a bond
  The gold of weight they lead out of the land!

GOOD COUNSEL: It is short time since any benefice
  Was sped in Rome, except great bishopries.
  But now for an unworthy vicarage.
  A priest will run to Rome in pilgrimage.
  A numbskull who was never at the school
  Will run to Rome and keep a bishop's mule,
  And then come home with many coloured crack,
  With a burden of benefices on his back—
  Which is against the law, one man alone
  For to possess more benefices than one.
  So I conclude, my lords, and say for me
  You should annul all this plurality!
  Advise, my lords, what think you to conclude?

LORD: Sir, by my faith, I think it very good
  That from henceforth no priests shall pass to Rome.
  Because our substance they do still consume.
  Also I think it best by my advice
  That each priest should have but one benefice.

GOOD COUNSEL: Mark well, my lords, there is no benefice
  Given to a man, but for a good office!
  Who take office, and then they cannot use it,
  Giver and taker, I say, are both abusèd.
  A bishop's office is to be a preacher,
  And of the Law of God a public teacher.

BISHOP: Friend, where find ye that we should preachers be?

GOOD COUNSEL: Look what Saint Paul writes unto Timothy.
  Take there the Book; let see if you can spell!

(*He hands Bible to* BISHOP.)

BISHOP: I never read that, therefore read it yoursel'!

(BISHOP *casts it away.*)

MERCHANT: Then before God, how can you be excusèd,
  To have an office and know not how to use it?
  Wherefore were given you all the temporal lands,

And all these tithes you have among your hands?
They were given you for other causes, I ween,
Than mumble matins and keep your clothes clean!
You say to the Apostles that you succeed,
But you show not that into word nor deed!

JOHN: King James the First, Roy of this region,
Said David was a sore saint to the crown.
I hear men say that he was something blind,
That gave away more than he left behind.

ABBOT: My lord Bishop, I marvel how that ye
Suffer this carl for to speak heresy!
For by my faith, my lord, will you take tent,[1]
Deserves he for to be burnt incontinent!
You cannot say but it is heresy
To speak against our law and liberty!

(*There is a great commotion. The* SPIRITUAL ESTATE
cry, " Burn him! " CORRECTION *intervenes and
addresses* JOHN.)

CORRECTION: Show forth your faith and feign it not!

(JOHN *pauses before saying his creed*.)

JOHN: I believe in God that all has wrought,
And created every thing of naught;
And in his Son, our Lord Jesu,
Incarnate of the Virgin true;
Who under Pilate tholèd passion,
And died for our salvation;
And on the third day rose again,
As Holy Scripture showeth plain.
Also, my Lord, it is well kennd,
How he did to the heaven ascend,
And set him down at the right hand
Of God the Father, I understand,
And shall come judge on Doomesday . . .
What will you more, sir, that I say?

CORRECTION: Show forth the rest: this is no game!

JOHN: I trow Sanctam Ecclesiam. . . .
But not in their bishops nor their friars!

MERCHANT (*to* CORRECTION): I think, my lord, if good it so
appears,
That the King's grace shall give no benefice

———
[1] note

But to a preacher that can use that office.
The silly souls that are Christ Jesus' sheep
Should not be given to gourmand wolves to keep!
What is the cause of all the heresies
But the abusion of the prelacies?

LORD: We think your counsel is very good,
As you have said we all conclude!

POOR MAN: Oh, my lords, for the Holy Trinity,
Remember to reform the consistory!

PARSON: What cause thou, false robber, for to plain ye?

POOR MAN: Therein I happened among a greedy menyie![1]
I lent my gossip my mare to fetch home coals
And he her drowned into the quarry holes!
They gave me first a thing they call citandum,
Within eight days I got but libellandum,
Within a month I got ad opponendum,
In half a year I got interloquendum,
And then I got—how call you it?—ad replicandum:
But I could never a word yet understand him!
But ere they came half way to concludendum
The fiend a plack[2] was left for to defend him.
Of pronunciandum they made me wonder fain,
But I got never my good grey mare again!

LORD: My lords, we must reform the consistory laws,
Whose great defame above the heavens blows!
So that the King's honour we may advance,
We will conclude, as they have done in France.
Let spiritual matters pass to Spirituality,
And temporal matters to Temporality!

(VERITY *and* CHASTITY *now press their complaint.*)

VERITY: My sovereign, I beseech your excellence,
Use justice on Spirituality,
The which to us has done great violence,
Because we did rehearse the verity;
They put us close into captivity,
So we remained into subjection,
Into languor and calamity
Till we were freed by King Correction.

CHASTITY: My lord, I have great cause for to complain,
I could get no lodging into this land;

[1] pack   [2] devil a halfpenny

The Spiritual State had me so at disdain.
With Dame Sensual they have made such a bond,
Among them all no friendship, sirs, I found:
And when I came the noble nuns among,
My lusty Lady Prioress from hand,
Out of her dorter dourly she me dang!

CORRECTION: What say you now, my lady Prioress?
How have you used your office, can you guess?
What was the cause you refused harboury
To this young lusty Lady Chastity?

PRIORESS   (*haughtily*): I do my office after use and wont!
To your Parliament I will make no account!

(*The* FIRST SERGEANT *steps forward and pulls her
from among the* SPIRITUAL ESTATE.)

FIRST SERGEANT: Come on, my Lady Prioress,
We shall learn you to dance,
And that within a little space
    A new pavane of France!

(*The* SERGEANTS, *in pulling her habit, haul it off and
show a gay dress underneath.*)

SECOND SERGT.: Now brother, by the Mass,
    By my judgment, I think
This holy Prioress
    Is turnèd a cow-clink!

PRIORESS: I give my friends my malison,
That me compelled to be a nun,
    And would not let me marry!
It was my friendes greediness
That made me be a Prioress,
    Now heartily them I wary![1]
Howbeit the Nuns sing night and days,
Their heart wots not what their mouth says,
    The sooth I you declare,
Making you intimation
To Christes congregation,
    Nuns are not necessair!
But I shall do the best I can,
And marry some good honest man,
    And brew good ale in tun!
Marriage, by my opinion,
                [1] curse

It is better religion,
>Than to be friar or nun!

(CORRECTION *now turns to* FLATTERY, *who is in the
stocks, still disguised as a friar.*)

CORRECTION: Sergeant, I counsel you from hand,
Banish yon friar out of this land,
>And that incontinent!
Yon flattering knave, without a fable
I think he is not profitable,
>I know his false intent!

SERGEANT: Come on, Sir friar, and be not fleyit,[1]
The King our master must be obeyed,
>But you shall have no harm.

(*He takes* FLATTERY *out of the stocks.*)

If you would travel from town to town,
I think this hood and heavy gown
>Will keep your wame[2] o'er warm!

(*He pulls off* FLATTERY'S *habit, so that the motley
is revealed.*)

GOOD COUNSEL: Sir, by the Holy Trinity,
This same is feignèd Flattery,
>I know him by his face!
Believing for to get promotion,
He said his name was Devotion,
>And so beguiled your grace!

FLATTERY: My lords, for God's sake, let not hang me,
Howbeit these widdiefows[3] would wrong me!
>I can make no debate
To win my meat at plough or harrows . . .
But I shall help to hang my marrows,
>Both Falsehood and Deceit!

CORRECTION: Then pass thy way and graith[4] the gallows!
Then help for to hang up thy fellows,
>Thou gets no other grace!

(*The gallows are brought in.*)

DECEIT: Now Flattery, my old companion,
What does yon King Correction?
>Knows thou not his intent?
Declare to us of thy nouvelles!

[1] frighted   [2] belly   [3] gallows worthy   [4] rig

FLATTERY:	You'll all be hangèd, I see naught else, And that incontinent!
DECEIT:	Now waylaway, will you cause hang us? The deil brought yon curst King among us, For meikle sturt and strife!
FLATTERY:	I had been put to death among you, Were it not I took in hand to hang you, And so I saved my life!
CORRECTION:	With the advice of King Humanity, Here I determine with ripe advisement, That all these prelates shall deprivèd be!
KING:	As you have said, but doubt it shall be! (*The* COURTIERS *lay hands on the* PRELATES.)
WANTONNESS:	My lords, we pray you to be patient, For we will do the King's commandement!
BISHOP:	I make a vow to God, if you us handle You shall to hell be curst with book and candle! (*The* SPIRITUAL ESTATE *is despoiled.*) We say the Kings were greater fools than we, That us promoted to so great dignity!
ABBOT:	There is a thousand in the Church, but doubt, Such fools as we, if they were well sought out! Now brother, since it may no better be, Let us go sup with Sensuality! (*They go to* SENSUALITY.)
SENSUALITY:	Pass from us, fools, by Him that has us wrought, You lodge not here, because I know you not!
GOOD COUNSEL	(*to* CORRECTION): Ere you depart, sir, off this region, Give John the Common-Weal a gay garmoun![1] Because the Common-Weal has been o'er lookèd, That is the cause that Common-Weal is crookèd. With singular profit he has been so suppressed, That he is both cold, naked and disguised.
CORRECTION:	As you have said, Father, I am content, Sergeants, give John a new habilament Of satin, damask, or of the velvet fine And give him place into our Parliament syne![2] (*Music. They clothe* JOHN *gorgeously and receive him into Parliament*.)
ESTATES	(*sing*): Salve, res publica!
POOR MAN:	I give you my broad benison, That has given Common-Weal a gown,

[1] garment   [2] then

But I beseech you, for All Hallows,
Cause hang Deceit and all his fellows,
And banish Flattery off the town,
For there was never such a loon!
(*The* SERGEANTS *take* DECEIT *and* FALSEHOOD *from
the stocks and lead them to the gallows*.)

FIRST SERGEANT: Come here, Deceit, my companion!
Saw ever a man liker a loon
    To hang upon a gallows?

DECEIT: This is enough to make me mangit![1]
Grief fall me that I must be hanged!
    Let me speak with my fellows!
I trow ill-fortune brought me here,
What meikle fiend made me so speedy?
Since it was said, it is seven year,
That I should wave into a widdy.[2]
I learned my masters to be greedy.
Adieu, for I see no remede.
Look what it is to be evil-deedy!

FIRST SERGEANT: Now in this halter slip thy head!
Stand still! Me thinks you draw aback!

DECEIT: Alas, master, you hurt my craig![3]

FIRST SERGEANT: It will hurt better, I would a plack,
Right now when you hang on the knag![4]

DECEIT: Adieu, my masters, merchant men,
I have you servèd, as you ken,
    Truly, both air[5] and late!
I say to you, for conclusion,
I dread you go to confusion,
    From time you lack Deceit,
I taught you merchants many a wile,
The upland wives for to beguile
    Upon a market day;
And make them trust your stuff was good,
When it was rotten, by the Rood,
    And swear it was not so!
I was aye whispering in your ear,
And taught you for to ban and swear
    What your gear cost in France,
Howbeit the Devil a word was true!
Your craft if King Correction knew,
    Would turn you to mischance!
I taught you wiles manifold—
To mix the new wine with the old,
    That fashion was not folly!

---

[1] deranged   [2] gallows   [3] neck   [4] gallows   [5] early

To sell right dear and buy dirt-cheap,
And mix rye-meal among the soap,
    And saffron with oyldolly.[1]
Forget no usury I pray you
More than the Vicar does the cow,
    Or lords their double-mail.
Howbeit your ell-wand be too scant,
Or your pound-weight three ounces want,
    Think that but little fail!
You young merchants may cry alas
For wanting of your wanted grace,
    Yon curst King you may ban!
Had I lived but half a year,
I should have taught you crafts perqueir
    To beguile wife and man!

SECOND SERGT.:   Come here, Falsehood, and grace the gallows!
You must hang up among your fellows,
    For your cankered condition!
Many a true man have you wronged,
Therefore but doubt you shall be hanged,
    But[2] mercy or remission!

FALSEHOOD: Alas, must I be hangèd too?
What meikle devil is this ado?
    How came I to this, cummer?[3]
My good masters, you craftsmen,
Want you Falsehood, full well I ken
    You will all die for hunger.
Find me a Webster[4] that is loyal,
Or a Walker[5] that will not steal!
    Their craftiness I ken.
Or a Miller that has no fault,
That will steal neither meal nor malt,
    Hold them for holy men!
At our Fleshers take you no grief,
Though they blow lean mutton and beef,
    That they seem fat and fair.
I taught Tailors in every town,
To shape five quarters in one gown,
    To them I taught that lore!
Adieu, my masters, Wrights and Masons,
I need not teach you any lessons,
    You know my craft perqueir!
Adieu, Blacksmiths and Loriners,[6]
Adieu, ye crafty Cordiners,
    That sells the shoon o'er dear!

[1] olive oil   [2] without   [3] gossip   [4] weaver   [5] fuller   [6] saddlers

Among craftsmen it is a wonder,
To find ten loyal among a hunder,
    The truth I to you tell!
Adieu, I may no longer tarry,
I must pass to the King of Fairy,
    Or else straightway to hell!
Farewell, for I am to the widdy[1] wend!
For why? Falsehood made never better end.

(DECEIT *and* FALSEHOOD *are hanged, to a Roll of
Drums.*)

FLATTERY: Have I not 'scaped the gallows well?
Yea, that I have, by sweet Saint Gile,
    For I had not been wrongit,
Because deserved I, by All Hallows,
To have been marshalled with my fellows,
    And high above them hanged!
I made far more faults than my mates,
I beguiled all the Three Estates,
    With my hypocrisy.
Mark well! My mates the piper pay,
But Flattery slips clean away,
    Of all the world I'm free!

(*Music.*)

DILIGENCE: Famous people, heartily I you require
This little sport to take in patience.
We trust in God, if we live another year,
Where we have failed, we shall do diligence,
With more pleasure to make you recompense,
Because we have been some part tedious,
With matter rude, denude of eloquence,
Likewise, perchance, to some men odious.
Now let each man his way advance!
Let some go drink, and some go dance!
Minstrels, blow up a brawl of France!
    Let see who hobbles best!
For I will run, incontinent,
To the tavern, ere ever I stent.[2]
I pray to God omnipotent,
To send you all good rest!

Music. A dance, followed by a march, during which
EXEUNT OMNES.

THE END

    [1] gallows   [2] stop